EARLY CHILDHOOD EDUCATION SERIE

Leslie R. Williams, Editor

ADVISORY BOARD: Barbara T. Bowman, Harriet K. Cuffaro,
Stephanie Feeney, Doris Pronin Fromberg, Celia Genishi, Stacie G. Goffin,
Dominic F. Gullo, Alice Sterling Honig, Elizabeth Jones, Gwen Morgan

(Continued)

SECOND EDITION

Understanding Assessment and Evaluation in Early Childhood Education

Dominic F. Gullo

TEACHERS
COLLEGE
PRESS

Teachers College, Columbia University
New York and London

Published by Teachers College Press, 1234 Amsterdam Avenue, New York, NY 10027

Library of Congress Cataloging-in-Publication Data

Gullo, Dominic F.
    Understanding assessment and evaluation in early childhood education / Dominic F. Gullo — 2nd ed.
        p.   cm. — (Early childhood education series)
    Includes bibliographical references and index.
        ISBN 0-8077-4533-2 (cloth : alk. paper) — ISBN 0-8077-4532-4 (pbk. : alk. paper)
        1. Educational tests and measurements—United States.   2. Early childhood education—United States—Evaluation.   I. Title.   II. Early childhood education series (Teachers College Press)

    LB3051.G85 2005
    372.12'64'0973—dc22   2004051794

ISBN 0-8077-4532-4 (paper)
ISBN 0-8077-4533-2 (cloth)

Printed on acid-free paper
Manufactured in the United States of America

12 11 10 09 08   8 7 6 5 4 3 2

Contents

v

PART IV
ASSESSMENT AND EVALUATION WITH SPECIAL POPULATIONS
OF CHILDREN   131

Preface

UNDERSTANDING THE role of assessment and evaluation in early childhood education is a complex process. There are vast numbers of children in early childhood programs who could be affected by assessment and evaluation. Whether the effect is positive or negative could ultimately be determined by the early childhood teacher's understanding of the process. Understanding the process of assessment and evaluation in early childhood involves understanding when and how to use assessment and evaluation; understanding how the child's development affects the process; and understanding the relationship between assessment, evaluation, and a curriculum that is developmentally appropriate for the child. Some of the understanding is just common sense, but some requires formal and deliberate learning on the part of the early childhood professional. It requires going beyond conventional wisdom and good intentions, for good intentions and conventional wisdom may lead to inappropriate practices.

CHANGES FOR THE SECOND EDITION

Since the first edition of this book was written, the landscape of early childhood education, assessment, and evaluation has changed in significant ways. With the advent of the No Child Left Behind Act, testing, accountability, and standards are words that are in the minds of all educators today, including early childhood educators. Questions arise as a result of these changes: How does the focus on testing and accountability affect assessment practices that we know are appropriate (or inappropriate, for that matter) for young children? How do we assess young children's attainment of academic standards when we know that the time it takes to attain these standards is different for each child? How do we demonstrate that programs are effective when the measures of effectiveness don't match the curriculum? These are just a few of the questions that the second edition of this book will address.

The children who are in our early childhood classrooms no longer look like the children who were in these classrooms when the first edition of the book was written. The number of children who come from culturally or linguistically diverse backgrounds has increased dramatically. Specific issues related to the assessment of these children have been of great concern to early childhood professionals. In this second edition of the book, a chapter has been added that addresses those issues related to the assessment of children who come from culturally and linguistically diverse backgrounds (Chapter 11).

The number of children who have been identified as having special needs and who are included in regular classrooms has also increased since the first edition of this book was written. This is largely due to changes in laws and changes in our ability to identify children who have special needs at earlier ages. This change also comes with specific challenges for teachers. One of the challenges stems from teachers' ability to use assessment information to inform curriculum practice for these children. Thus a chapter on issues related to children with special needs has also been added to this edition as a means of helping teachers better understand the relationship between assessment, curriculum, and instruction for this population of children (Chapter 10).

In addition to these two new chapters, another new chapter has been added in which a more detailed description of the psychometric characteristics of standardized assessments is discussed (Chapter 5). With the advent of increased uses of standardized assessments for various purposes, it is important that teachers and other practitioners who work with young children understand these characteristics.

Other significant changes in the current edition include both an expanded annotated list of assessment instruments covering readiness tests, achievement tests, developmental screening tests, and diagnostic tests and a glossary of terms associated with assessment, evaluation, and curriculum and instruction in early childhood education. The chapter on integrating alternative assessment procedures into the early childhood curriculum has also been expanded to include charts that will help teachers and other early childhood professionals understand the possibilities of assessing children's knowledge and skills as they are engaged in various types of curriculum activities.

OVERVIEW OF THE CHAPTERS

The book is divided structurally into four parts. In Part I, issues concerned with the unique relationship between the field of early childhood and assessment and evaluation will be introduced and discussed. In Chapter 1, an overview of issues related to assessment and evaluation in early childhood is given. Included in this discussion are historical and legislative influences affecting assessment and evaluation. Chapter 2 discusses issues related to the role of assessment and evaluation in early childhood. Topics include principles and purposes of evaluation and assessment in early education and the manner in which evaluation and assessment are processes integrated into the curriculum and instruction of early childhood programs. Development is the primary topic of Chapter 3: Developmental characteristics of children are described, along with the ways these characteristics may affect children's test-taking behaviors.

Part II of the book focuses on formal assessment and evaluation in early childhood education. Chapter 4 describes the various types of standardized instruments that are appropriate in early childhood and how to decide which to use. Psychometric characteristics of tests are presented in Chapter 5. The particular importance of validity, reliability, and practicality for early education is explained, as are statistical concepts and terminology. Chapter 6 discusses the advantages and disadvantages of standardized assessments as well as the possible negative impact on children, curriculum, and professional trends. Suggestions for overcoming these shortcomings are presented.

The main focus of the three chapters in Part III is informal assessment and evaluation procedures that are commonly used in early childhood education settings. In Chapter 7 various types of informal assessment and evaluation procedures appropriate for use in early childhood settings are described, and their advantages and disadvantages are discussed. Topics in Chapter 8 include defining alternative assessment, types of alternative assessment, and strategies for developing an alternative assessment program. In Chapter 9, ways to incorporate alternative assessment into the various early childhood curricular areas are described.

In Part IV of the book, assessment and evaluation issues related to special populations of young children are the focus. In Chapter 10, assessment issues related to children who are identified as having special educational needs will be discussed. Chapter 11 will focus on assessment of children who come from backgrounds that are culturally and linguistically diverse.

Acknowledgments

MUCH GOES into the writing of the second edition of a book and with it goes gratitude to many. I'd like to thank the reviewers for their insightful suggestions on how to bring the second edition up to date and in line with the changing climates in early childhood education and assessment. Their comments were truly a guide.

Once again, I'd also like to give sincere thanks to Susan Liddicoat. She is insightful, encouraging, and has the gift of seeing things that those who are too close to the project have difficulty seeing.

I could not have completed this project without the support of my family. Support sometimes can be translated to "putting up with me." To my sons, Matt and Tim, thank you for bringing joy into my life . . . and bringing me back to reality whenever you sensed I needed it. To my wife, Jeanne, I cannot express enough gratitude for allowing me to follow my dreams.

Finally, to Joe, thank you so much for teaching me how to assess only those things that are significant in life, and how to not dwell in the past, but live in the present and look forward to the future.

Understanding Assessment and Evaluation in Early Childhood Education

PART I

Introducing Assessment and Evaluation in Early Childhood Education

CHAPTER 1

Assessment and Evaluation in the Early Childhood Years

A CHILD IS born! Within the first 60 seconds of life it is determined that the newborn has a heart rate of 120 beats per minute, she entered the outside world crying vigorously and breathing regularly, she withdrew her arms and legs when touched, she vehemently rejected the efforts of others to straighten her limbs, and her skin seemed to glow from the top of her head to the tip of her toes. Her score: 10.

From the moment of birth, assessment and evaluation play an important part in our lives. The illustration above is an often-repeated scene in hospital delivery rooms throughout the United States today. During the first minute of life, infants are observed and assessed, and their Apgar score is determined. Five minutes later, another Apgar score is established. The Apgar Scale (Apgar, 1953) is a widely used assessment instrument that rates the newborn's physical well-being. Scores can range from zero to ten with a high score indicating good physical condition. The score provides a quick and valid indication of the need for possible and/or immediate intervention in the areas of respiration, circulation, pulmonary functioning, and other sensorimotor functions.

In 1904 the French minister of education recognized the need for a classification system to assist educators in admitting, placing, and developing educational programs for children entering special schools. As a result, a special commission was appointed in Paris to study the situation. A psychologist by the name of Alfred Binet was a member of this commission. By 1905 the Binet Scale was developed and used as an educational placement instrument by French schools (Kelley & Surbeck, 1983). The educational testing movement had begun!

The Binet Scale and the Apgar Scale demonstrate two aspects of assessment and evaluation in early childhood. Assessment and evaluation have been around for a long time, and they begin early in the lifetime of an individual.

Recently, in the field of early childhood education, there has been an ongoing debate related to the various roles that assessment and evaluation play within the profession. This debate has focused on what types of assessment and evaluation are appropriate for young children and what uses and misuses can result from the outcomes of these evaluations. Most of this debate has focused specifically on the misuses of standardized testing in early childhood education (see, for example, McAfee & Leong, 2002; Meisels & Atkins-Burnett, 2004; Mindes, 2003; Worthen & Spandel, 1991).

While much of the current focus in the debate is on standardized testing issues, it is important to look beyond. The process of assessment and evaluation is more than simply testing and measuring. Understanding children's performances or academic or behavioral competencies involves more than looking at their test scores. It is more than comparing one child's scores to those of other children in the same grade or developmental level. It is important to know and understand what underlies those scores, that is, what may have influenced the child's performance and resulted in a particular score on a particular test. This is especially true in early childhood education due to the qualitative differences in children's thinking at this stage as compared with later stages of development.

It is essential that professionals who work with young children really understand the constructs underlying assessment and evaluation in early childhood so they can make appropriate decisions regarding the selection of assessment instruments and methods. And, given the results of assessment procedures, they need to be able to make informed and appropriate decisions about children and curriculum. The issues surrounding testing and measurement in early childhood have become complex. Appropriate use (or misuse) of assessment and evaluation information can influence the direction of an individual child's or group of children's early, as well as later, education and developmental trajectories. This book's purpose is to help early childhood practitioners develop the essential understanding they require and to illuminate many of the issues involved in assessment and evaluation.

PARAMETERS OF EARLY CHILDHOOD

In order to establish a common frame of reference regarding the period of development referred to as early childhood, it is necessary to define its use in this book. Early childhood can be described from three different but related perspectives: chronological age, developmental stage, or traditional school grade level.

Chronologically, early childhood is defined as ages birth to 8 years old. These are the years of greatest dependency on others, and according to some (Scarr, 1976), the period of greatest biological similarity with respect to the course of development, particularly cognitive development. In addition to recognizing that this age span consists of many universal developmental traits, it has also been recognized as being uniquely different from ages beyond the 8th year. There is, in fact, a biophysical change in the brain that occurs at around age 7 or 8 (Anastasiow, 1986). The maturation and resulting integration of particular brain functions at this age make it possible for children to learn things at age 7 or 8 that were not possible at age 5.

The developmental definition of early childhood is understandably very closely related to the chronological definition. According to Piaget (1963), a developmental child psychologist whose work has significantly influenced and shaped the field of early childhood education, the parameters of early childhood are captured by the sensorimotor and preoperational periods of cognitive development. These two stages of cognitive development include approximately the first 8 years of life and are characterized by the unique manner that children use to process information, construct knowledge, and solve problems. As a result, children in this developmental period require specialized instruction and learning environments.

Children whose developmental timetables are either accelerated or delayed best illustrate differences between the chronological and developmental definitions of early childhood. Children who are chronologically beyond the early childhood years, but whose cognitive development is within the preoperational stage, do better when taught with techniques and materials appropriate for early childhood education. Conversely, some early childhood education strategies may not be appropriate for children beyond the preoperational period, but whose age falls within the defined early childhood years.

Finally, early childhood can be defined by grade level (National Association of State Boards of Education [NASBE], 1988). This is particularly appropriate in the school setting. Early childhood education covers those grade levels between prekindergarten and third grade. Increasingly, more and more schools are including prekindergarten as part of their regular academic programs. These programs generally start at age 4; however, some may begin as early as age 3.

Early childhood education generally refers to programs appropriate for children ages birth to 8 years old. These programs may be housed in various locations, ranging from private facilities (e.g., child care centers, preschools, hospitals) to agencies (e.g., Head Start), to public school programs.

ASSESSMENT AND EVALUATION: DEFINING THE TERMS

Now that the parameters of early childhood have been established, it is important to define some general terminology that will be used in the discussion of assessment and evaluation throughout the book. The terms and concepts defined here will not be related to specific assessment or evaluation techniques, as these will be defined in later chapters in an appropriate context. Rather, the terminology presented here represents concepts that are pertinent across the wide array of issues related to assessment and evaluation.

Assessment

Assessment is a procedure used to determine the degree to which an individual child possesses a certain attribute. The term *assessment* can be used interchangeably with *measurement*. According to Boehm (1992), there are several purposes for assessment in early childhood.

One purpose for assessment is to gain an understanding of a child's overall development. This would be helpful for the teacher in order to identify those areas where specific help or teaching is required. Identifying emerging areas of development and pinpointing those areas already possessed would provide information useful in determining a child's readiness for instruction and would aid in identifying the appropriate forms and levels of classroom instruction.

Another purpose for assessing an individual child is for the teacher to gain a better understanding of how the child is progressing within the program. In doing so, teachers can advance their knowledge concerning the diverse learning styles and strategies used by various children. In addition, the collective assessments of children's academic achievement can be used to measure the effectiveness of programs and interventions.

A final reason for assessing individual children is to identify those who are at risk for academic failure or are potentially in need of special education services. Such assessment procedures may begin as screening and lead to further in-depth evaluation or diagnosis, including the evaluation of environmental factors that influence both learning and development.

Mindes (2003) offers a thorough description of assessment in early childhood:

Assessment is a process for gathering information to make decisions about young children. The process is appropriate when it is systematic, multidisciplinary, and based on the everyday tasks of childhood. The best assessment system is comprehensive in nature, that is, the assessment yields information about all the developmental areas: motoric, temperament, linguistic, cognitive, and social/emotional. (p. 10)

Mindes goes on to say that, although there are many definitions of assessment, there are common elements or characteristics that they all share: Assessment is a process; assessment is used as a decision making tool; assessment can be applied to either an individual or to a group of children; and assessment results in the generation of products.

Assessments can be either formal or informal in nature. Academic readiness tests, developmental screening tests, and diagnostic tests are all types of formal assessments, most of which are standardized tests. Standardized tests are those that allow one to compare the performance of an individual child on a test to that of other children who have similar characteristics. Information from individual assessments may be combined in education evaluation procedures. Informal assessments include such things as performance assessment, portfolio assessment, developmental or academic checklists, and anecdotal records. Both formal and informal assessment will be discussed more thoroughly in later chapters.

Evaluation

Evaluation is the process of making judgments about the merit, value, or worth of educational programs, projects, materials, or techniques. Assessments may be used during the process of educational evaluation in order to make these judgments. Evaluation often includes researchlike techniques, for the judgments and conclusions derived from evaluation are based upon evidence (Smith & Glass, 1987). Evidence can include both systematic as well as unsystematic observations of program outcomes.

Evaluations can either be comparative or noncomparative, according to Smith and Glass. In a comparative evaluation, alternative programs' outcomes are assessed and compared. In a study by Gullo, Bersani, Clements, and Bayless (1986), for example, kindergarten programs using either a half-day, full-day, or alternate full-day schedule were compared to determine their relative effects on children's academic achievement and classroom social behavior. The relative benefits of alternative programs can be assessed by comparative evaluation techniques, and decisions regarding these programs can be made based upon empirical evidence.

In noncomparative evaluation, program outcomes are assessed in one group only, and these results are compared with an absolute criterion (Smith

& Glass, 1987). For example, Head Start programs are evaluated using the Program Review Instrument for Systems Monitoring (PRISM). PRISM includes criteria for meeting program standards for each of the components in the Head Start program (American Institutes of Research, 2003). Reasons for program noncompliance are provided for each program criterion. For each area of the program not in compliance with the standards, a strategy for meeting criteria must be developed.

Similarly, the National Association for the Education of Young Children (NAEYC; 1985) has established the National Academy of Early Childhood Programs. This is an evaluation approach based upon criterion standards used for accrediting early childhood programs. In this evaluation, different components of an early childhood program are compared with standards developed by NAEYC. Accreditation by this organization has become a nationally recognized standard of quality.

In NAEYC's position statement, *Early Childhood Curriculum, Assessment, and Program Evaluation* (2003), it is suggested that a number of guidelines should be considered when making decisions regarding individual child assessment and program evaluation. These include answering the following questions:

1. What is the purpose of evaluation in early childhood programs?
2. What is accountability?
3. What standards of quality should be used in evaluation programs that serve young children?
4. Is it necessary for all programs serving young children to be evaluated?
5. What components should a program evaluation include?
6. Who should conduct program evaluations?
7. What kinds of support are needed in order to conduct a good evaluation?
8. How should data gathered in a program evaluation be analyzed?
9. How should information from a program evaluation be used? (pp. 15–16)

Alternative Assessment

Alternative assessment refers to an assessment option that focuses on methods other than strict adherence to the standard tests-and-measurement paradigm. *Authentic assessment* (Chittenden, 1991) and *portfolio assessment* (Shanklin & Conrad, 1991) are terms sometimes used interchangeably with *alternative assessment*. According to Chittenden (1991), although nomenclature varies, the goals of alternative assessment appear to be consistent. The first goal of alternative assessment is to incorporate actual classroom work into individual assessment. Secondly, a critical goal of alternative assessment procedures is to enhance both children's and teachers' participation in the assessment process. Finally, alternative assessment attempts to meet some of the accountability concerns of school districts and funding agencies.

HISTORICAL CONTEXT OF ASSESSMENT AND EVALUATION IN EARLY CHILDHOOD

Assessment and evaluation in early childhood education have evolved through the years, in respect to the reasons for doing them and the manner in which they are accomplished. Both have often evolved out of mandate, rather than out of practicality for better understanding the development and learning processes in young children. Assessment and evaluation in early childhood have their roots in the child study movement, advances in the development of psychometric practices, as well as in legislative mandates (Wortham, 2001). A brief look at these influences will provide a necessary context for understanding assessment and evaluation in early childhood today.

The Child Study Movement

The child study movement emerged after the turn of the twentieth century. The scientific study of the child was initiated by Darwin, who suggested that the development of the infant mirrored the development of the human species (Kessen, 1965). Darwin's theory of the development of the species spawned a great deal of interest in scientifically and methodically studying children's development. Following Darwin's lead, G. Stanley Hall became a primary influence in advancing the scientific methods for the study of children and created a center for that purpose at Clark University. Hall's students were John Dewey, Arnold Gesell, and Lewis Terman, each of whom went on to make major contributions to the field of child study (Irwin & Bushnell, 1980; Wortham, 2001). The focus of each of these men's special interests uniquely contributed to the child study movement.

Gesell's interests were in the chronological development of children. He painstakingly described the emergence of different types of child behaviors in chronological sequence. His main emphasis was on maturation, and he believed that maturation led development. The term *milestones* was used to describe the average age at which particular behaviors would emerge. The sequence of development within a particular category was invariant according to a maturationist's perspective. Any differences in the timing of the emergence of particular behaviors from child to child was seen as individual differences in maturation.

John Dewey's primary scientific focus was on the education of children. He was a major influence in the educational reform movement that resulted in changes in the development of educational programs for young children. At the University of Chicago, Dewey was chairman of a department that combined psychology, philosophy, and education (Cleverley & Phillips, 1986). As a result, Dewey published in all three areas and at the same time became interested in the laboratory school that was on the university campus. He became a driving force in the progressive movement, which began as a movement in social reform "but quickly came to focus upon educational change as a practical way of improving society" (p. 107).

Terman, who was a professor at Stanford University, became interested in the Binet Scale, a measure that was designed to identify and differentiate children who were normal and those who had mental disabilities. In 1916, Terman published a revised version of the Binet Scale, which became known as the Stanford-Binet. Terman introduced the term *intelligence quotient* with the publication of the newly standardized Stanford-Binet (French & Hale, 1990).

The War on Poverty

In the 1950s there was a growing concern regarding the consistently lower academic performance among children who came from homes of economic poverty. As many researchers began investigating this phenomenon, there was increased national interest in developing programs for children who came from low socioeconomic backgrounds to decrease the disparity between their academic achievement and that of their middle-class counterparts (Wortham, 2001). As a result, massive amounts of federal dollars were allocated for the development of programs for poor children. A "war on poverty" was waged, and Head Start became the primary educational program for poor preschool children.

Many models of programs were developed during this time (White, 1973; Zigler & Valentine, 1979), and a necessary component in all programs was program evaluation. As a direct result, new measures had to be developed to assess children's progress, the primary purpose of which was to evaluate the effectiveness of the programs in which they participated (Laosa, 1982). The evaluation research that was conducted as a result of the Head Start mandates was uneven at best, as were the instruments that were developed to measure children's progress. However, the assessment instruments and evaluation processes that were developed because of Head Start contributed greatly to the growing field of assessment and evaluation in early childhood education (Hoepfner, Stern, & Nummedal, 1971). The growing need to assess children and evaluate programs because of federal mandate resulted in constant improvement of assessment instruments and evaluation procedures (Wortham, 2001).

Legislative Influences

Beginning in the 1960s, there were a number of legislative acts that greatly influenced assessment and evaluation. Much of this focus was on young children with disabilities.

PL 94-142. The Education for All Handicapped Children Act (Public Law 94-142) was passed in 1975 and proved to be one of the most significant influences in the assessment of young children. At the heart of the law was the guarantee of equal education in free public school settings and in the least restrictive environment for all children aged 3–21 with disabilities. In order to accomplish this goal, the law also mandated that all children be assessed with nondiscriminatory tests (McCollum & Maude, 1993).

The assessment instruments that existed at the time were not considered adequate to test, diagnose, and place students who had various types of disabilities. The law also required that a team of individuals with different areas of expertise assess the children and make decisions regarding appropriate placement. As such, multiple points of assessment became a means to accomplish this. Because there were great variations in the types of disabilities that children had, assessment for the purpose of diagnosis and placement became the greatest challenge (Mehrens & Lehmann, 1991). These legislative mandates led to many new assessment instruments as well as new assessment and evaluation strategies and processes.

PL 99-457. The Education of the Handicapped Act Amendments (Public Law 99-457) was passed in 1986 as a way of addressing the shortcomings of PL 94-142. Under the new law, two early childhood programs were established: the Federal Preschool Program and the Early Intervention Program. Under PL 94-142, individual states could decide whether or not they would provide services to children between the ages of 3 and 5; but under PL 99-457, states must demonstrate that they are providing services to children between the ages of 3 and 5 if they are to receive the federal monies provided under PL 94-142. The Federal Preschool Program extended the rights of children between the ages of 3 and 5 under PL 94-142.

The Early Intervention Program went beyond the Federal Preschool Program and extended services to children with developmental delays who were between the ages of birth and 2. All of the states who participated in PL 94-142 had to provide services to infants and toddlers who demonstrated developmental delays (McCollum & Maude, 1993; Meisels & Fenichel, 1996).

As a result of PL 99-457, the challenge became how to assess very young children with disabilities and evaluate the effectiveness of their programs (Cicchetti & Wagner, 1990). This challenge led to an increase in the development of instruments and procedures used to assess infants, toddlers, and preschoolers with disabilities. Because both public laws discussed thus far required the participation of a wide variety of individuals, it became necessary that they become familiar with the assessment strategies used to identify and place young children with disabilities (Goodwin & Goodwin, 1993). A lot of challenges faced professionals who served young children with disabilities. In particular, the evaluation of the effectiveness of programs designed for these children proved to be most difficult (Wortham, 2001).

PL 101-576. The Americans with Disabilities Act (ADA) (Public Law 101-576), passed in 1990, had a profound impact on the education of young children. The ADA provides that all programs serving young children must be prepared to serve children who are identified as having special needs. Its amendments to PL 94-142 mandated that the individual educational needs of all children with special needs be met in early childhood programs (Deiner, 1993; Wolery, Strain, & Bailey, 1992). As a direct result of this, the term *mainstreaming* was replaced with *inclusion* (Krick, 1992). This led to further advances in the study of assessment and evaluation in that children had to be assessed and programs had to be evaluated in order to determine whether or not individual children's needs were being met and whether or not the programs were effective.

As can be seen from this brief description of the historical context for assessment and evaluation in early childhood, there were many influences emanating from many sources. Understanding the roots of assessment and evaluation is helpful for grasping the underlying reasons for the directions that the evolution of assessment and evaluation took.

Today there are still other forces shaping the direction of assessment and evaluation in early childhood. These include such things as school and teacher accountability, the standards movement, and the No Child Left Behind Act. These will be the topics of discussion in Part II of this book.

GUIDING THEMES FOR THIS BOOK

In this book, three themes will emerge and guide the discussion of understanding assessment and evaluation in early childhood. These themes will provide the underlying conceptual framework, both theoretical and philosophical, for the topics presented.

Development and Evaluation

First and foremost, the central theme will focus on the consideration of the child's developmental stage and characteristics, and how these factors relate to assessment and evaluation procedures and outcomes. The focal question here is, how does one use assessment to formulate appropriate questions that will elicit appropriate answers? The premise for this question is that assessment is a means of determining what the child knows, what the child can and cannot do, what knowledge or information the child has acquired as a result of a particular experience, to what degree the child can appropriately use the information he or she has acquired, and so on. In order to ask the right kinds of questions to determine these things, educators have to be able to match words, situations, pictures, activities, objects, gestures, and other types of stimuli to what children, given their stage of development, can meaningfully process. If such a match exists, one can expect that the response given by the child will reflect his or her understanding. If the match does not exist, then the response may not reflect the child's actual level of competence in the particular area being assessed.

Effect of Assessment and Evaluation on Children

Another theme that will be important to many of the discussions in this book is the effect that assessment and evaluation have on the child. In part, this is a validity and reliability issue; that is, is what is being assessed being accurately measured? The question lies not so much in the psychometric properties of the assessment or evaluation instruments (see Chapter 5)—assessment and evaluation need not even involve instrumentation—but rather in the validity and reliability of the process being undertaken to make certain decisions.

Again, it is necessary to return to a developmental principle. A fundamental premise of stage theories in child development is that while all children proceed through the same stages of development in the same sequence, not all children proceed at the same rate. This can be noted particularly in the areas of cognitive development and language, two aspects of child development often assessed in early childhood education. Another feature of this type of developmental sequence and rate is that by the time all typically developing children reach the age of 8, many of the individual differences observed earlier, related to rate of biological maturation, have evened themselves out (Anastasiow, 1986; Gullo, 1992).

If educators evaluate children and use this information as an indication of their future academic potential or use it inappropriately to group children into homogeneous ability groups, the differences that will result in children's academic environment as a result of these evaluations could be dramatic. When labels are attached to children—primarily the result of assessment findings that are invalid for these purposes—most children will perform according to the categorical labels that have been associated with their assessed performance. In the case of homogeneous ability groups, the experiences that children have or don't have in the "lower" groups will inhibit them from "moving up" to the "higher" ability groups. This is true even when children's later developmental levels indicate that they could have met the behavioral expectations of the latter group.

Relationship Between Curriculum and Evaluation

Another assessment and evaluation validity issue that is integrated throughout this book is the importance of the match between what is being assessed and what is occurring within the curriculum. Broadly speaking, the early education *curriculum* can be defined as a set of experiences that can occur in almost any setting in which children happen to be engaged in activity. It is not limited to a *classroom* in the formal sense of the word. The curriculum experience includes the physical setting, the materials, the specific content, and the social and physical interaction. Within this issue, two topics must be considered, both concerned with the relationship between curriculum and evaluation.

First, the relationship refers to the parallel structure that should exist between what is being evaluated and what is being presented vis-à-vis the curriculum. In order to be valid, there should be a close match between the curriculum and evaluation instrumentation. Curriculum here refers to both content and methods.

A second topic that will be considered regarding the curriculum and evaluation relationship has to do with influence. Two questions will be discussed: Should curriculum influence what evaluation techniques and materials will be used? Should the evaluation influence what and how the content of the curriculum should be taught?

Curriculum and evaluation comparability. Although an individual is assessed to determine academic and curricular performance or competence, the process of individual assessment occurs within the context of the curriculum. As such, the specific evaluation or assessment content and procedure should reflect the curricular content and instructional strategies that are being utilized. If the curriculum is implemented using one set of assumptions and evaluated using others, children's performance may not reflect what they have actually attained as a result of participating in the curriculum. This is especially true for young children, who by their developmental nature have a difficult time generalizing knowledge and performance from one context to other contexts.

A good example of this is the correlation, or lack of it, between how reading and math are often taught in early childhood education, and how reading and math performance is evaluated. The teaching of reading and math may focus on process rather than on the attainment of isolated skills. The whole-language approach to reading/language/writing and the manipulative-math approach to arithmetic are good examples of process-oriented teaching strategies. In both of these instructional strategies, it is not the "right" answers that is the focus of instruction, but rather the problem-solving strategies that are used to reach the answers. Both approaches emphasize using divergent problem-solving strategies, multiple probable responses, and individualized timetables for reaching mastery.

But a problematic and critical consequence that has arisen from process-oriented early education curricula is that it may be difficult to reliably evaluate the processes involved in these types of instructional strategies. Because of this, many schools are relying on "traditional" assessment instruments and evaluation techniques even though these are usually product oriented with an emphasis on the right answer. In addition, an implicit assumption is that all children being assessed should be developmentally at the same place at the same time. As a result, evaluation findings often do not accurately reflect children's actual competence resulting from curricular experiences. This may precipitate the misconceptions that the curriculum is not effective or that the children are not competent in acquiring the curricular content.

Evaluation and curriculum—an influential relationship. A question that seems to be part of every inquiry, scientific and nonscientific, is, which came first? This question is appropriate here. It is important to remember that evaluation should be used as a tool to measure and determine any number of attributes relative to the individual or the curriculum. Thus one should be cognizant of the characteristics of the curriculum in selecting assessment procedures. Evaluation should not determine curriculum content or strategies. Rather, curriculum should determine which type of assessment instruments and strategies should be used.

Implications. These two aspects of the relationship between evaluation and curriculum overlap but have different effects. The first one, related to comparability, may affect what teachers may believe about children's competence. If the assessment materials or procedures are not comparable to the curriculum and a student's score is low, the teacher may believe that the student is not doing well. The second topic, related to influence, may affect the curriculum content or instructional strategies. If children do not do well on assessment instruments that are not well matched to what is being taught or how the content is delivered, teachers may be inclined to "reconstruct" the curriculum so that there is a closer match, rather than maintaining the curriculum and selecting a new method of assessment or evaluation.

These three themes—the relationship between evaluation and child development, the effects of assessment and evaluation on children, and the relationship between curriculum and evaluation—will be apparent throughout this book, although they will not necessarily be reiterated explicitly in each chapter.

CHAPTER 2

Putting Early Childhood Assessment and Evaluation in Perspective

AS STATED in Chapter 1, the process of assessment and evaluation constitutes more than simply testing and measuring. In most test and measurement textbooks, general psychometric properties of tests and measurements are discussed, and readers are cautioned to take these characteristics into consideration when making decisions about which measurements to use for what purposes and in what situations. These characteristics are to be considered in the construction of teacher-made tests as well. While these considerations are important and can be generally applied to most students in educational settings, early childhood education presents a somewhat different scenario.

During most of the early childhood years, it is difficult to measure and assess bits of knowledge and skills that are isolated from other types of knowledge and skills. Young children are not reliable test takers due to the many different confining personal, developmental, and environmental factors that affect their behaviors (this notion will be expanded upon in Chapter 3). In addition, just as children do not develop in an isolated manner, they do not acquire knowledge nor learn specific bits of information or skills without learning other things within the contextual framework. As a result, measuring whether children have acquired specific information may be a somewhat difficult, invalid, and unreliable task if teachers view the assessment and evaluation process as being a similar one across the various age, developmental, and grade levels.

Another difficulty arises out of the situation that is prevalent in many discussions of tests and measurements: It is assumed that the test taker is a reader. This is understandably not the case for most of the children in early education settings. Therefore, alternative means of assessing children must be used, although alternative procedures and materials come with their own problems. Questions related to reliability, validity, predictability, and generalizability are often raised. In addition, comparability problems surface.

In this chapter, following the presentation of background information, three facets of assessment and evaluation in early childhood education will be discussed: general principles guiding assessment and evaluation in early childhood; purposes for assessment and evaluation in early childhood; and viewing assessment and evaluation as part of the educative process. Recent issues related to early childhood assessment are integrated into these discussions where appropriate, including high-stakes testing, formal versus informal procedures, accountability and assessment, and assessment with special populations of children.

THE ASSESSMENT CLIMATE FOR EARLY CHILDHOOD

"By the year 2000, all children will come to school ready to learn" (U.S. Department of Education, 1991). This was Goal 1 of the National Education Goals—the first education goal set by the nation's governors at a meeting in Charlottesville, Virginia, in 1990. It was intended to respond to the needs of children, but right from the start, it led to much controversy over what should be put into place to make sure that children were indeed ready to learn when they started school. An erroneous assumption embedded within this goal was that some children started school *not* ready to learn. Validation for this assumption came from the interpretation of assessment information that was used in determining a child's readiness for school, and from the definition of *readiness* that was being used. The definition of readiness cannot be separated in reality from assessment practice. Explicitly, the practice of how an individual uses assessment data, along with the assumptions that one makes related to what measurement tells us about a child's readiness status, lead to the determination of whether a child is assessed as ready for school or not (Gullo, 1997).

Goal 1 also led to the development of educational standards for young children by professional organizations (McAfee & Leong, 2002). After that, every state in the United States developed standards for children from kindergarten through Grade 12 and mandated assessment for the purpose of determining if children were meeting those standards (Meisels, 2000). While most states had no mandated testing until the end of third grade, many states began testing in kindergarten.

Advisors to the National Education Goals Panel for Goal 1 could not find an appropriately valid and reliable method for assessing young children before they entered formal schooling (Shepard, Kagan, & Wurtz, 1998). In 1994, the advisors were charged to "create clear guidelines regarding the nature, functions, and uses of early childhood assessments, including assessment formats that are appropriate for use in culturally and linguistically diverse communities, based on model elements of school readiness" (p. 3). This charge to the advisory panel led to the development of general principles and purposes guiding assessment and evaluation practices in early childhood.

GENERAL PRINCIPLES FOR GUIDING ASSESSMENT AND EVALUATION PRACTICES IN EARLY CHILDHOOD

The Goal 1 advisory panel to the National Education Goals Panel, also known as the Goal 1 Early Childhood Assessments Resource Group, developed six early childhood assessment principles that were designed to guide policy maker's decision-making process for both policy as well as practice. These principles are included in the report to the National Education Goals Panel submitted by the Goal 1 Early Childhood Assessments Resource Group (Shepard, Kagan, & Wurtz, 1998; quoted principles are from this source).

Principle 1: Benefit Children

The first principle states that "assessment should bring about benefits for children" (p. 5). Gathering assessment information that is accurate for making decisions about children can be a time-consuming and stressful process. It also is potentially a very costly process, one that can take resources away from programs and the services that they provide for children. The time taken way from programs in order to implement the assessment procedure also has the potential for taking direct services away from children. To merit this, it should be clearly demonstrated that the assessment would result in providing clear benefits for children. This can be either in the form of improvements to the quality of the programs in which children participate or in an increase in the amount of direct services that are provided for children.

Principle 2: Be Used for a Specific Purpose

Principle 2 states that "assessments should be tailored to a specific purpose and should be reliable, valid, and fair for that purpose" (p. 5). All assessments, especially standardized assessments, are designed for a single purpose; if they are used for other purposes, they are not valid, and the result is often the abuse or misuse of the testing findings. The decisions based on much of the high-stakes testing today reflect the misuse of tests. Assessments must be used only for their intended purposes. The principles that follow address these issues.

Principle 3: Recognize the Limitations of Young Age

According to the third principle, "assessment policies should be designed recognizing that reliability and validity of assessments increase with children's age" (p. 5). The primary tenet of this principle is that the younger the child, the more difficult it is to obtain reliable and valid results from assessment procedures. This is especially true in the assessment of children's cognitive abilities. It is cautioned that many types of assessments should not be administered until the child is older. If assessments are administered to younger children, appropriate safeguards should be taken in both the administration and interpretation of the findings.

Principle 4: Be Age-Appropriate

The fourth principle states that "assessments should be age-appropriate in both content and the method of data collection" (p. 6). Assessment procedures should be used in a manner that recognizes that children develop and learn in a wide variety of ways. Assessments should address all areas of learning and development including cognitive development, language development, physical development and well-being, social and emotional development, and motor development. In addition, assessments should address a variety of approaches to learning as well as general knowledge. In order to demonstrate their abilities, children need contexts that are familiar to them. For this reason, assessments should be conducted in settings that are familiar to young children and in which they feel comfortable. Young children are also concrete learners and thinkers. Paper and pencil tests are abstract by their very nature and often are not useful in allowing children to demonstrate what they know.

Principle 5: Be Linguistically Appropriate

According to Principle 5, "assessments should be linguistically appropriate, recognizing that to some extent all assessments are measures of language" (p. 6). When assessing young children both their first and second language development should be taken into consideration. If a child is one who comes to school with limited English proficiency, all assessments—

regardless of their stated purpose—become assessments of the child's proficiency in English. Thus the child's language should be taken into consideration when determining assessment tools and procedures. The results of any type assessment may be confounded by the child's language. A more in-depth examination of this issue will be the focus of Chapter 11.

While the Early Childhood Assessments Resource Group did not specifically address cultural appropriateness, I feel that it is important to say a word about it here. Young children in this country come from very diverse backgrounds—culturally, linguistically, ethnically, racially, and socioeconomically. These differences among children, who are often in the same classroom, can and will affect the assessment process as well as the validity of the assessment. Standardized assessments are often particularly criticized for their lack of sensitivity to the various backgrounds from which children come (McAfee & Leong, 2002). According to McAfee and Leong, it is important to recognize that teachers also come from their own sociocultural backgrounds. If teachers understand their own sociocultural backgrounds, they are more likely to be sensitive to the differences found among the children in their classrooms (Frank, 1999). It is important to recognize that children's individual backgrounds will have a significant influence on the kinds of knowledge they amass, the vocabulary that they develop, and the skills that they learn. All of these differences may affect the process and outcomes of assessment.

Principle 6: Value Parents

Principle 6 states that "parents should be a valued source of assessment information, as well as an audience for assessment results" (p. 6). As a result of many of the assessment limitations that have been discussed above, parents should be viewed as an important source of information regarding their child's development and learning. In addition, assessment procedures should be such that they provide valuable information to parents concerning their child's development, learning, achievement in school, as well as the progress that is being made by their child. Parents should be viewed as an integral part of their child's education.

Many people equate standardized testing with assessment and evaluation. As such, standardized tests are generally administered at the end of an educational experience, and the test results are used for many purposes—some appropriate, some inappropriate. Teachers often fear testing because it implies that they are the ones being evaluated. While schools should be held accountable for learning, using assessment and evaluation findings as a means of determining whether one teacher is teaching better than another is not an appropriate use of evaluation results. While teacher accountability and appropriate use of evaluation can be compatible, the information gleaned from individual assessments and program evaluation should be used to reflect and inform the educative process rather than to force it into arbitrary quality categories.

PURPOSES FOR ASSESSMENT AND EVALUATION IN EARLY CHILDHOOD EDUCATION

As stated earlier, assessment and evaluation reflect more than simply standardized testing, and there are numerous reasons for assessing children and evaluating programs, all of which are related. The Goal 1 Early Childhood Assessments Resource Group developed four general purposes for assessment and evaluation (Shepard, Kagan, & Wurtz, 1998; quoted purposes are from this source).

Purpose 1: Assessment to Support Learning

The first purpose, "assessing to promote children's learning and development" (p. 9), advocates that the process of teaching and the process of assessment are inseparable. Individual assessment is crucial to determine the starting point from which to begin the curriculum process with children. Typically, two aspects are considered within this framework. The first is the usefulness of determining what type of academic skills and factual knowledge the child has. Academic skills are the types of knowledge and problem-solving abilities children have as a direct result of experiencing curriculum activities. Academic skills are needed to continue or progress through the curriculum sequence. These include such things as knowledge of number, conceptual knowledge, logical knowledge, factual knowledge, and so on. According to Meisels (1987), readiness tests might be one useful tool in determining the child's current level of academic functioning, and he maintains that readiness tests can be used to assist teachers in planning the curriculum. In addition, information from readiness tests can help teachers determine how prepared children are to engage in particular curricular activities and therefore whether they can benefit from them. While readiness tests can be a useful tool in determining children's relative academic functioning and preparedness, cautions accompany their use.

There are other less formal means of determining children's academic functioning. Observing children engaged in activities is very useful in determining their level of functioning within academic settings. Talking with them and asking questions is another. Cryan (1986) lists a number of informal techniques of assessing academic readiness in children, including direct observation, interviews, checklists, samples of children's work, and anecdotal records. Used systematically, such methods will provide the teacher with much useful information.

The second aspect of assessing children is to determine their current level of developmental functioning. Knowledge about children's motor development, language development, and cognitive development is essential for teachers to design appropriate curriculum activities. Another reason to ascertain children's current level of developmental functioning is to determine whether they might benefit from alternative curricular experiences. A developmental screening test may help provide this information. According to Meisels (1987) and Meisels and Atkins-Burnett (1994), developmental screening tests can be used to help identify children who may need further diagnostic testing to determine whether they require intervention or special education services. Further, Meisels indicates that by identifying children's levels of developmental functioning, teachers may better understand those children who are in need of a modified or individualized curriculum. Again, there are cautions in administering, interpreting, and applying the results from these instruments.

Purpose 2: Identification of Special Needs

The second purpose, "identifying children for health and special services" (p. 15), states that assessment should also be used to identify children's special problems for the purpose of determining if there is a need for additional services beyond that which is already provided. Special needs are described as blindness, deafness, speech and language disabilities, cognitive delays, emotional disturbance, learning disabilities, and motor impairment.

Usually a two-step process is required to identify children with special needs. The first step is screening. This is a very brief assessment to determine whether further assessment is warranted. Screening is only used during the initial stages of special needs identification and referral. Often, classroom teachers or others who have no special training in the administration of standardized diagnostic assessments administer screening assessments.

If it is determined that further assessment is needed in order to ascertain the nature of the special need, a diagnostic procedure is implemented. The child is referred to the appropriate specialist or specialists who assess the child in depth using diagnostic assessments. Specialists include such individuals as the school psychologist, speech pathologist, medical doctor, a counseling psychologist, and the like. In many cases a team of individuals rather than just one specialist does the diagnostic procedure. The outcome of the diagnostic procedure is twofold. First, the assessment procedure should identify the nature of the special need or needs. Second, and just as important, the diagnostic procedure should indicate the type of program that will best serve the child's needs. Assessing children who are identified as having special educational needs is the focus of Chapter 10.

Purpose 3: Child Progress and Program Evaluation

In the third purpose, "monitoring trends and evaluating programs and services" (p. 23), individual child assessments are combined across groups of children to determine program effectiveness and examined individually over time to examine children's progress. According to McAfee and Leong (2002), there are three reasons for teachers to track children's progress. First, teachers need to know that what they are doing with children in the classroom results in learning and development. Second, teachers need to show both families and children that progress is being made. And third, by providing evidence of progress to children and families, an increase in motivation on the part of both parents and children may be realized. Teachers should use ongoing assessment in order "to understand specific children and to gain information on which to base immediate decisions on how to direct, guide, teach, or respond" (Phinney, 1982, p. 16).

By combining assessment information from the children in the classroom, teachers can also evaluate the effectiveness of their program while it is in progress. Evaluation with this purpose is often referred to as *formative evaluation*. Formative evaluation refers to assessments of quality that are focused on curricular programs that may still be modified. Following a program's design and implementation, formative evaluation is undertaken to assess the program's progress as well as to provide information that could lead to the program's improvement (Royce, Murray, Lazar, & Darlington, 1982). The major purpose of formative evaluation is to determine whether or not the curricular goals and objectives are being met.

According to Wortham (1990), many different aspects of the early education experience can be monitored through formative evaluation. These include equipment and materials used to implement the curriculum, specific curriculum activities, and teachers' behaviors during the implementation process. At the heart of the formative evaluation strategy is the gathering of evidence regarding the efficacy of the various components of the curricular and instruction sequences, and the consideration of this evidence in order to isolate the probable deficits and to suggest possible modifications. The specific strategies used during formative evaluation in early education settings may be of a formal or informal nature.

Specific instruments have been designed to evaluate different components of the early education program. For example, the early childhood environment can be evaluated and monitored using an instrument designed by Harms, Clifford, and Cryer (1998). The revised edition of the

Early Childhood Environment Rating Scale (ECERS-R) can be used by classroom teachers to assess children's personal care routines, furnishings and displays for children, language-reasoning experiences, fine and gross motor activities, creative activities, social development activities, and adult needs. Each of the factors in the environment are rated on a scale from 1 (inadequate) to 7 (excellent). At rating points 1, 3, 5, and 7, a description of the characteristics for the factor at that rating point is given.

In addition, Louise Derman-Sparks (1989) has developed strategies for identifying bias in early childhood programs. In her book she identifies different types of bias and the ways in which bias can occur in early education settings. She discusses racial bias, cultural bias, gender bias, and stereotyping in general. Derman-Sparks elaborates on how bias can occur within the environment, materials, books, and activities found in the early childhood program. She also discusses ways the curriculum can be evaluated for bias and provides strategies for modifying the curriculum to eliminate it.

Talan and Bloom (2005) provide administrators with a means of evaluating whether the administrative characteristics of their programs indicate good early childhood programming. They cover a number of administrative concerns, including staff orientation, supervision and performance appraisal, staff development, compensation, benefits, staffing patterns and scheduling, facilities management, risk management, and internal communications.

As can be seen, the primary objective of formative evaluation is to modify the program to enhance it. Formative evaluation should take place on a continuing basis during the implementation life of the program, rather than at the end of the program when modifications would not be beneficial to those completing the program.

On the other hand, determining the effectiveness of an educational experience at its conclusion is called *summative evaluation*. In summative evaluation, information is gathered regarding the worth of an overall instructional sequence so that decisions can be made regarding whether to retain or adopt that sequence. This sequence can either be a specific one (e.g., balanced literacy instruction or basal reading instructional approach) or one that represents a whole-program approach (e.g., full-day kindergarten or half-day kindergarten schedule).

Take, for example, the question of deciding between a half-day or full-day kindergarten schedule—a dilemma that many school districts are facing. Obviously there are advantages and disadvantages to both. In a summative evaluation, the evaluator would be interested in determining if the benefits of a full-day kindergarten schedule warrant either keeping a full-day schedule or changing to it from the more traditional half-day schedule. At the end of the school year, the summative evaluation might investigate what effects the full-day kindergarten schedule (as compared with the half-day kindergarten schedule) has on a number of variables: end of the year general achievement levels, reading levels, depth of curriculum coverage, parent satisfaction, child attitudes toward school and learning, teacher satisfaction, retention, attendance, social development, ease of transition into first grade, and so forth. With this kind of information, the task of deciding whether to retain or adopt the full-day kindergarten schedule is made easier, and the decision would be based on more objective evidence.

In summative evaluation, the end of an educational sequence is somewhat arbitrary. For example, in making the decision of whether to adopt a full-day kindergarten schedule, the end of the instruction sequence could be put at the end of the kindergarten year or it could be put at the end of third grade, which is often identified as the end of early education (Bredekamp, 1987; Gullo, 1992). An evaluator might decide on the latter if it is anticipated that some of the effects of the full-day kindergarten may not reveal themselves until later in a child's educational experience.

Another example of when defining the end of the curriculum at different times might be appropriate would be in assessing the relative benefits of using a "balanced literacy" approach to reading. While balanced literacy strategies are used widely in prekindergarten and kindergarten, the rate that children develop and demonstrate various reading skills under this system may differ from those children who focus on the specific and isolated reading skills that are emphasized more in a basal approach to reading instruction. Therefore, the end of kindergarten or first grade may not be the appropriate time to evaluate this approach and compare it to the reading skills approach. While children using the balanced literacy approach will eventually consolidate these skills, it may not be until the end of second grade or the beginning of third grade that a valid appraisal of the child's reading ability can be obtained using traditional reading assessment instruments.

While summative evaluation is important in making curricular decisions, one must make the appropriate determination of when it should occur. Formative and summative evaluation should go hand in hand. Formative evaluation offers information on how curriculum could or should be modified to make it more efficacious, while summative evaluation elucidates the overall effectiveness of the experience.

It is important to point out that when assessments are aggregated in such a manner, they should be used for evaluating the effectiveness of programs. They should not be used, in this instance, for making curricular decisions about individual children who participate in these programs (Shepard, Kagan, & Wurtz, 1998).

Purpose 4: Accountability

"Assessing academic achievement to hold individual students, teachers, and schools accountable" (p. 29) is the fourth purpose for assessing children in early childhood programs. As was stated earlier, all states have developed standards for children's performance in Grades K–12. Individual assessments can also be combined in order to determine whether or not these standards are being met, thus holding schools to a measure of accountability.

Two types of standards are usual in this instance. *Content standards* are one type of standards that have been developed. Content standards refer to *what* should be learned within the various subject areas. Content standards can also include critical thinking ability, problem solving skills, reasoning, and strategies that are used by children in gathering information (McAfee & Leong, 2002).

Performance standards refer to the levels of achievement that are thought to be appropriate for individual grade levels. They are a means of determining the degree to which content standards have been achieved (Lewis, 1995; Ravitch, 1995). Most performance standards include benchmarks for each grade, indicating the level of attainment that children should have for each of the content standards (McAfee & Leong, 2002). It is anticipated that as children progress through the grades, their level of knowledge and skills will increase accordingly for individual subject areas.

The early learning standards position statement developed by NAEYC (2002) is a specific example of how standards apply to young children and combine issues relevant to both content standards and performance standards. In the position statement it is stated that early learning standards are a valuable component in a comprehensive program for young children to insure quality programs and future academic success. These results can only be guaranteed if the following conditions are present: (1) Programs should emphasize content and outcomes that are significant and developmentally appropriate; (2) learning standards are developed and reviewed through a process that reflects current understanding of children's learning; (3) the assessment of the attainment of these standards should be accomplished by using assessment strategies that are both ethical and appropriate for young children; and (4) the learning standards should reflect strong support for early childhood programs, families, and professionals.

ASSESSMENT AND EVALUATION AS PART OF THE EDUCATIVE PROCESS

It should be evident from the above discussion, which delineates the various reasons for assessment and evaluation in early childhood education, that assessment and evaluation are a large part of the process of educating the child. Assessment and evaluation should not focus solely on outcome measures that are directed toward behaviors identified as success markers. Rather, they should be viewed as dynamic processes, integral to and subject to curriculum development and implementation. As such, assessment and evaluation can be described as educative processes having three distinct characteristics: continuity, comprehensiveness, and integration.

Continuous Process

Assessment and evaluation are continuous processes. One primary focus that describes assessment and evaluation processes in early childhood education is that they should be procedures that describe the progress of children over time. One cannot define what progress is, or describe it, if evaluation is limited to assessing children only at the end of their experiences. By conceptualizing assessment and evaluation as continuous processes, the conceptualization of how children learn is implicitly affected as well. There is no inherent beginning, middle, or end to children's learning. While it may be important to identify the sequence that children are learning, what is also significant to recognize, and subsequently measure, is that children are progressing through the sequence, not necessarily that they are all at the same point in the sequence at some given moment. Education evaluation and assessment should be viewed as a description of where children are at any given moment within some learning sequence continuum. It is important to recognize, as well, that just as time continues on, so too does learning and the assessment of learning.

Comprehensive Process

Assessment and evaluation are comprehensive processes. Recall the story of the five blind men who experienced an elephant for the first time. After they had a chance to touch the elephant for a moment, each described to the rest of the group what he thought the elephant must look like. The first blind man, who touched only the elephant's leg, thought that the elephant must look like a tree. After all, its skin was as rough as the bark of a tree and body as thick as a tree's trunk. After feeling the elephant's trunk, the second blind man was convinced that an elephant must look like a snake. It has no apparent skeletal structure and could move in wavelike motions. The third blind man, touching the elephant's ears, conveyed to the rest that he thought the elephant must look like a large fan. The fourth man said the elephant must look like a long rope, after feeling the tail. The last blind man, feeling the large body of the elephant, described the elephant to the other four men as a large round boulder.

What does this story tell us about the assessment of children and program evaluation? While none of the men were totally wrong, none of them were totally right in their descriptions of the elephant. Each of them was partially correct because each only partially experienced the elephant. While assessing young children and evaluating early education programs are much more complex processes than describing an elephant, there are some similarities. Not only are there many aspects of learning and development that can be assessed, there are also many contexts within which they can be assessed. It is important to understand that evaluation should utilize multiple sources of information, assess multiple aspects of the individual, and take place in multiple contexts.

This issue relates to a critical characteristic of assessment and evaluation in early education settings—the multidimensional aspect of learning and development, and of the environments in which they occur. According to James Comer (1999),

> Children's . . . development depends on relationships. . . . relationships are to development what location is to real estate: We need relationship, relationship, relationship. The best instructional methods, curricula, and equipment are not going to produce good outcomes in bad relationship environments, which are found most often where students, parents, and staff are all underdeveloped or unable to express their abilities and potential. (p. xxiv)

Integrative Process

Evaluation and assessment are integrated into the instructional process. The instructional goals expressly stated in the curriculum should guide the process of evaluation. The nature of what is assessed and how assessment procedures are defined should be directly linked to the experiences children have within the curriculum. As will be discussed in Chapter 8 on "alternative assessment," assessment and evaluation procedures can be subsumed within the instructional process itself.

There are two ways that the outcomes of assessment and evaluation are directly linked to instruction. First, assessment and evaluation can be used as tools for modifying curriculum to meet individual children's needs. Since children benefit in different ways from different instructional strategies, evaluation can be used to determine which children benefit from which instructional strategies. Second, evaluation can be used as a tool to measure overall curriculum effectiveness. Just as curriculum experiences are beneficial to different children in different ways, there may be some curriculum experiences that are not effective for any children. Thus

evaluation can be a useful instrument in making general curriculum ad-
justments, as well as individualized ones.

In this chapter, the role of assessment and evaluation in early childhood
was discussed from various perspectives. It was described as having various but related purposes and characterized as a process, integrated into
curriculum development, implementation, and modification. Particular
attention was given to the general purposes and principles guiding assessment and evaluation in early childhood education that were developed
in response to national concerns about education that surfaced in the
1990s. These should help determine whether the curriculum and assessment processes that are employed will lead to early learning that is appropriate. In Chapter 3, the relationship between early child development
and assessment will be described.

Evaluation from a Developmental Perspective

I N THE 1920s and 1930s it was commonly assumed that infants were blind or at least minimally sighted at birth. One of the leading reasons for this belief was that behavioral scientists at the time were not very good at "asking questions" of infants and often applied assessment techniques that were appropriate for older children. When the infant "failed" these tests, the assumption was either that the behavior did not exist or the infant was incapable of performing the behavior. Not until infant development and behavioral competencies were better understood were more developmentally appropriate and therefore more accurate assessment techniques created. While this represents a blatant example of a mismatch between the child's development and the assessment technique, more subtle instances exist in early childhood as well.

One of the primary ways that preschool children are evaluated is through the use of teacher-directed questions. In a study of teacher-child discourse Blank and Allen (1976) found that up to 50% of the language that teachers use in the classroom are teacher-posed questions. Conventional wisdom was that if children did not answer the question appropriately or at all, they did not know the right answer. A number of studies have found that there is, in fact, a developmental sequence that determines the types of questions children can comprehend (Cairns & Hsu, 1978; Gullo, 1981; Tyack & Ingram, 1977). The following order has been established: *yes-no* questions; *who* questions; *what* questions; *where* questions; *when* questions; *why* questions; and *how* questions. This order represents increasing levels of abstractions required to comprehend what type of information is being requested.

For example, the concepts related to *who, what,* and *where* are concrete referents related to persons, places, and things. These are concepts that children acquire early. On the other hand, concepts related to *when, why,* and *how* are abstract concepts related to time, cause-effect relationships, and manner, respectively. These are concepts that children acquire later, sometimes not until 6, 7, or 8 years old. Yet teachers assume many times that "all questions are created equal" and do not selectively choose the types of questions they ask when assessing young children.

It was also found in a subsequent study (Gullo, 1982), that the order of questions listed above also represented increased levels of linguistic complexity required to respond appropriately to the question. To respond appropriately to the earlier developing questions (*yes-no, who, what, where*), a single word response is acceptable and appropriate (e.g., *yes* or *no,* a person, a thing, a place). To answer *when, why,* or *how* questions, children need to formulate more complex linguistic utterances to respond appropriately. The implication is that younger children, even if they know the information that is being requested of them, may not have the complex linguistic structures needed to answer the questions being asked.

The two examples described above—infant assessment and preschool question comprehension—illustrate the importance of child development and its relationship to individual assessment. They show just how development can and appropriately should influence the process of assessment. Conversely, they also demonstrate the erroneous conclusions that may be drawn from assessment results if the child's development is not considered.

In an assessment policy statement, the National Association for the Education of Young Children (1988a) states, in essence, that early childhood practices should reflect and take into account the child's level of development. Likewise, it should be recognized that the developmental characteristics of children affect assessment and evaluation procedures and outcomes (Cryan, 1986; Gullo, 1988, 1992; Meisels, 1987). The manner in which this principle impacts curriculum development and implementation is well documented (see, for example, Bredekamp & Copple, 1997; Gullo, 1992). It is imperative, however, that the assessment and evaluation procedures and processes be considered an integral part of the curriculum in the early childhood classroom.

DEVELOPMENTAL CHARACTERISTICS

Under both formal and informal assessment and evaluation conditions, it should be recognized that the developmental characteristics of individual children, or the characteristics of a group of children within a particular developmental period, affect how they will respond in and to various assessment and evaluation situations. In this section, four such developmental considerations will be discussed.

Developmental Constraints on Responses

First, there may be developmental constraints influencing children's responses in certain assessment situations. When children in early childhood settings are assessed in order to determine whether or not they have acquired specific information during a particular instructional experience, it should not be assumed that an inappropriate response or no response at all indicates that they do not have the sought-after information. One of the things that should be considered if this occurs is whether or not the method used to assess the child is consistent with the child's individual and general age-related developmental capabilities to respond.

If, for example, the assessment method requires that the child use extremely controlled fine motor movements (e.g., fill in a small bubble on a sheet with many pictures and other bubbles), the inability to exhibit movements such as these may actually impede the child's ability to demonstrate that he or she has acquired the knowledge being assessed. Similarly, the language used by an adult or another individual to assess a child's performance may not be consistent with the child's own level of language development, or the adult's language may not reflect content that is familiar because the child comes from a very different background. In this situation, the question is not meaningfully stated for the child, who will not respond in the anticipated manner even if the information or skill being assessed is known or has been acquired.

Another developmental trait of children during the early childhood years is that they demonstrate impulsive behaviors more than children who are at more advanced levels of development. Impulsivity means that children will often respond with the first thing that comes to their mind without reflecting on or considering alternative responses. This thinking without reflection leads younger children to respond in assessment situations in ways that are not consistent with adult expectations. Multiple-choice assessments using pictures provide a good illustration. One typical item on such an assessment might require a child to look at a picture and then circle one in a following row of pictures that goes best with the first. Typically, on items such as these, the test developers place a "decoy" picture first. This is a picture that would be the "best" response, if there wasn't a subsequent "better" choice. The young child might be disadvantaged with this type of test structure because he or she might select the first picture that meets the requirements of the task and never consider the choices that follow.

In summary, the children's level of social, language, cognitive, and motor development often affects how they will interpret and respond during both formal and informal assessment situations, and must be taken into account when their responses are interpreted.

Differences in Motivation

A second important developmental consideration is that the motivation to do well in evaluative situations differs depending on children's level of developmental accomplishments as well as on their experiential backgrounds. Experience with children and youths as well as research shows that motivation to do well accounts, in part, for a good performance in that situation. Young children often don't understand the importance or significance of their performance in these formal or informal assessment situations. Many times, the incentive to perform is simply to complete the task so that they can go on to a more comfortable or enjoyable circumstance. There is little that can be done, in general, to convince 5-, 6-, or 7-year-olds that their performance during certain evaluations may have long-range consequences on their academic future. Thus children's lack of motivation to perform according to external standards and expectations may influence their behavior in these situations.

There are some groups of children, however, who have more experience with assessment-like situations, and therefore may be more motivated at earlier ages than others to perform well. Children who come from middle-socioeconomic-status (SES) backgrounds are more likely to have been engaged in this type of situation than children who come from homes of economic poverty. Because they are more likely to have had this type of experience before, in their homes as well as in other types of settings, they may be more comfortable answering questions or being assessed in other ways. Familiarity alone could account for these children being more at ease and therefore more motivated to do well in an assessment situation.

Exaggerated Perception of Performance

A third developmental consideration is that there are differences between how children perceive themselves and how others perceive them relative to their performance on various tasks. An important element in the evaluation of children's performance is the degree to which they incorporate feedback into the internalized assessment of their own competence.

Research suggests that younger children's perception of their own competence is inconsistent with teachers' ratings of their competence (Gullo & Ambrose, 1987; Stipek, 1981). Teachers anticipate that the critical feedback given to children is used by the children to gauge future behaviors, but this is a misconception. It is not clear that young children, below the age of 8, perceive the feedback as criticism, or that they use teacher feedback focused on academic performance to determine or modify their future behaviors. Research has found that young children uniformly have an exaggerated perception of their own abilities (Gullo & Ambrose, 1987; Stipek, 1981). Nicholls (1978) found that it is not until sixth grade that children's perceptions of their abilities closely reflect their actual performance. Children's ratings of their own performance do not begin to correlate with teacher ratings of children's performance until about 8 or 9 years of age.

A developmental explanation for this phenomenon exists. From a Piagetian framework, Stipek (1981) concludes that preoperational children may confuse the desire to be competent with reality. Because most children do not get feedback regarding their competence that is either all good or all bad, they are left with mixed messages regarding their actual performance status. Preoperational children are then left to judge their own competency level based upon inconsistent and ambiguous feedback from the teacher.

Piaget (1925) describes children of this age as having an exaggerated feeling of self-efficacy. This may be due to the egocentric nature of the preoperational child. Children at this age tend to concentrate on and pay attention to that which is salient to them. When they receive evaluative feedback from the environment, both positive and negative, they may focus on only the positive, thus getting a false sense of competence. Apple and King (1978) suggest that teachers of young children tend to focus on school behavior and social adjustment when giving feedback to the children rather than provide reinforcement on the basis of the quality of the children's academic performance. Children may use this feedback to evaluate their competence in cognitive and academic performance as well. Thus young children may get little direct and meaningful feedback regarding their academic performance.

Differences in Generalizing Knowledge to New Concepts

The fourth developmental consideration is that there are differences in how children generalize their performance or knowledge from context to context. It is not appropriate to assume that because children's performance in academic settings indicates that they possess knowledge or skills within one particular context, that they will be able to generalize this knowledge or skill and demonstrate it in all contexts. This reflects a developmental phenomenon known as *vertical decalage* (Phillips, 1975). For example, if children are only provided with experiences using mathematical concepts and operations in contexts where they manipulate objects but never have experiences using representational symbols, these children may not be able to demonstrate what they know when assessed representationally with paper and pencil tasks. Therefore, it is imperative that children be given opportunities to experience knowledge and skills in many contexts, both concretely and representationally.

While it is true that children in the preoperational stage of development acquire new knowledge and skills when given concrete experiences with real objects, it is important that they be allowed to practice and generalize these newly acquired skills and knowledge in many different contexts. The implication here is twofold. First, that a child can demonstrate a competence in a particular context does not mean that the child has completely incorporated and internalized the understanding of this knowledge or skill enough to demonstrate it in all possible contexts. Conversely, that a child does not demonstrate a called-upon competency during an assessment situation does not mean that the child would not be able to demonstrate the knowledge, skill, or process if requested to do so in an appropriate context.

CHARACTERISTICS OF LEARNING ENVIRONMENTS THAT ARE DEVELOPMENTALLY APPROPRIATE

While it is imperative to consider the developmental characteristics of children when assessing them, it is also important to understand the importance of the characteristics of the learning environment. The learning environment should reflect developmental appropriateness so that learning and development can be optimized in children. Children learn and develop best in an environment that takes into account how children learn and develop naturally. Likewise, when assessing children, these same characteristics should be taken into consideration. If children's learning and development are optimized within such a context, so too assessment that occurs within such a context will yield more valid and reliable information about children. There are four characteristics of the learning environment that should be considered.

Hands-on Experiences

An environment that facilitates active learning through hands-on experiences optimizes learning and development in young children. Young children are active learners by nature. They learn and develop best when they have opportunities to manipulate concrete objects. During the learning process, children act on experiences and organize these experiences mentally (NAEYC, 1990). They construct their knowledge about the world through experiences that involve interactions with objects and people in their environment. Just as children learn in this manner, they reflect what they know when the assessment procedures mirror this type of activity. They are concrete thinkers and interactive learners; they are active thinkers and active learners. Procedures that allow children to demonstrate what they know in an active and interactive manner exemplify the kind of assessment that best reflects young children's capabilities.

Facilitation of Conceptual Learning

Environments that facilitate conceptual learning that leads to understanding and the acquisition of basic skills optimizes learning and development in young children. Children continually hypothesize about the world around them. According to NAEYC (1990), "children need to form their own hypotheses and keep trying them out through mental actions and physical manipulations—observing what happens, comparing their findings, asking questions, and discovering answers" (p. 6). Not until young children develop concepts in the broad sense are they able to acquire basic skills and knowledge about that which they hypothesize. If educators assess young children by asking them to demonstrate that they have acquired isolated bits of knowledge and skills, they are assessing children's ability to memorize and give back the right answers. With this method, educators may not know if the children have an understanding of the concepts behind the isolated bits of knowledge and skills.

Meaningful Context

An environment that facilitates learning in a meaningful and relevant context optimizes learning and development in young children. Young children are not abstract thinkers and learners; they require that what they learn be meaningful to their life experiences. Young children cannot extrapolate meaning from a context that has no meaning or relevancy in their lives. So too, children will demonstrate what they know if it is assessed in a meaningful way, within a meaningful and relevant context. The manner in which young children are assessed should reflect the kind of environment in which they learn.

Integrated Content

An environment that facilitates a broad range of relevant content that is integrated across traditional subject matter divisions optimizes learning and development in young children. Young children do not develop in one area at a time. Neither do they learn in this isolated manner. In most cases, assessment should not primarily focus on determining whether or not children have learned isolated bits of information. Assessment is more valid if it is done in such a manner that it can be determined how children use the knowledge that they have acquired in a variety of different ways and in a variety of different settings.

ASSESSMENT AND EVALUATION CONSIDERATIONS

When children are developing well, they learn well. When the adults in their lives show trust, support, positive regard, high expectations, affiliation, and bonding, learning comes naturally. But what happens when children aren't developing well, aren't learning well? What should we do when students don't do well in their schools? Some educators blame these children and their families, concluding that there is something inherently wrong with them. (Comer, Haynes, & Joyner, 1996, p. 1)

In this quote, Comer et al. were referring to broader issues related to educational systems. However, an important lesson can be gleaned from this statement with regard to assessment in early childhood education. The first error in making the assumption that children don't learn or can't learn is not knowing how to determine if they have learned. If they "fail the test," the conclusion is that they obviously haven't learned anything. Some children are more vulnerable to this faulty reasoning than others.

In this chapter, a number of developmental considerations have been discussed. The aim is for this information to shed new light on assessment, so that when children "fail the test," educators will think, "did we ask the right questions?"

The developmental and curricular principles and issues discussed in Chapters 1–3 are significant in assisting early childhood educators to make appropriate decisions regarding assessment and evaluation. There are many types of assessment and evaluation procedures available for use in early education settings. The type of procedure chosen by the early childhood educator should take into account a number of factors.

First, what is it that is going to be assessed? Some things are more reliably assessed using one procedure over another. For example, if a teacher is trying to determine the number of procedures or steps children take to solve a particular problem, this might be considered an assessment of a process, rather than a skill. It may be more appropriate to use a more informal assessment technique in this situation. If, on the other hand, a teacher is trying to determine what information children have already acquired in order to plan curriculum activities, a more formal technique may be appropriate.

Second, what are the children's developmental characteristics that will be assessed? How do these developmental characteristics relate to what is being assessed? As was discussed previously, the developmental immaturity of some children or the lack of linguistic or fine motor competence of others may preclude the use of some assessment techniques. The developmental characteristics of children must be taken into account when selecting assessment procedures and interpreting assessment results.

Third, what is the intended use of the assessment information? If the intended use is to describe certain behaviors or academic skills or processes, then the score from a more formal assessment procedure would probably not be appropriate. If, however, the intended use is for the determination of an individual's ranking on a particular skill or informational task, then a more formal assessment score may be the more appropriate avenue to take.

Fourth, who will be implementing the assessment procedure? Some assessment procedures require no specific training. Others require very specific training and skills. It must be determined if the person executing the assessment or evaluation procedure possesses the necessary skills to adequately accomplish the task.

PART II

The Role of Formal Assessment and Evaluation in Early Childhood Education

CHAPTER 4

Formal Assessment and Evaluation Instruments

FORMAL ASSESSMENT and evaluation instruments generally refer to standardized tests, which allow educators to compare an individual child's performance on the test to the performance of other children who have similar characteristics. In early childhood education, four types of standardized assessments are used: developmental screening tests, readiness tests, diagnostic tests, and achievement tests. These tests are appropriate to use in different situations.

GENERAL CHARACTERISTICS OF STANDARDIZED TESTS

Although there are different types of standardized tests, standardized test instruments have several format and procedural characteristics in common:

1. There is a specifically stated purpose. According to the American Psychological Association (1974), "the test manual should state explicitly the purpose and applications for which the test is recommended" and "should describe clearly the psychological, educational, and other reasoning underlying the test and the nature of the characteristic it is intended to measure" (pp. 14, 15).
2. There should be established procedures for administering and scoring the test. Any problems with administration or exceptions to the administration procedures should be clearly described.
3. There should be a description of how to interpret the test results.

The test manual should give clear directions on how to meaningfully compare an individual child's score with another's.

4. There should be a description of the sample population on which the experimental version of the test was developed. This is an important consideration. If the comparative scores on the test were based on a "white, middle-class, urban, upper midwest" sample, the comparison of an individual child's scores might be meaningless if the child comes from a largely "African American, lower socioeconomic, rural, southern" region. One should examine the test manual to determine if the sample used to develop the test is representative of the population at large, or appropriate for the specific population being tested.

5. Any limitations of the test should be stated in the test manual. Again, if the test was developed using a narrowly defined sample, it would be valid for use with children matching those characteristics but might have limitations when used with other types of children.

TYPES OF FORMAL ASSESSMENTS

In early childhood education there are many reasons to use formal assessments. The overall aim should be to inform curriculum and instruction. That is, from the information derived from the tests, more can be learned about the children, and this knowledge can be used for modifying the curriculum to meet individual children's needs. Four types of formal assessments and reasons for their use will be discussed in this section.

Developmental Screening Tests

According to Meisels and Atkins-Burnett (1994), developmental screening in early childhood education "is a brief assessment procedure designed to identify children who, because of risk of possible learning problem or . . . [special need], should proceed to a more intensive level of diagnostic assessment" (p. 1).

In a related article, Meisels (1987) states that there are primarily two purposes for developmental screening. The first is to identify those children who may be in need of special educational services. The second is to identify those children who might benefit from a specialized educational plan within the "regular" classroom. In this manner, a developmental screening test is used to measure children's potential for learning.

In their position statement on standardized testing of young children, NAEYC (1988a) states that developmental screening tests are inaccurately labeled as such and are in actuality "developmental tests." These two views are not dichotomous; they both wholly agree on two aspects. First, they agree that these tests measure certain skills and behaviors that children have already acquired. Therefore, such things as motor development, language development, and conceptual development might all be assessed on a developmental screening test. Second, they both agree that the results of developmental screening tests are often misused. This practice can lead to inappropriate placement of the child within the early childhood setting or, even worse, can prevent the placement of children in programs.

Generally, developmental screening tests are norm-referenced assessment instruments that allow one to compare an individual child's score with those of other children of similar chronological age (see Chapter 5). Many of the available developmental screening tests vary somewhat in their focus. Meisels and Atkins-Burnett (1994) state, however, that most of the test items on the screening instruments can be grouped into three areas.

In the first area, items are related to visual-motor and adaptive skills. These involve such things as control of fine motor movements, eye-hand coordination, the ability to recall sequences using visual stimuli, copying forms from two-dimensional representations of the form, and reproducing forms from a three-dimensional model.

The second area involves skills related to language/communication and thinking. The tasks here include language comprehension and expression, reasoning, counting, and recalling sequences from auditory stimuli.

The third area includes gross motor skills and body awareness. This involves such things as balance, coordination of large muscle movements, and body position awareness.

The greatest misuse of developmental screening tests stems from using instruments that are neither valid nor reliable (Meisels, 1987). Both reliability and validity will be discussed in Chapter 5. Suffice it to say for now that a reliable test is one that is consistent in what it measures, and a valid test measures what it purports to measure. Many of the developmental screening tests that are used are teacher-constructed instruments. These tests usually do not undergo psychometric research to establish their validity and reliability. Therefore, it is not always easy to accurately ascertain what the test measures.

While developmental screening tests that are both valid and reliable can measure children's learning potential, research has indicated that the ability to predict future school performance declines over a 2-year period (Meisels, Wiske, & Tivnan, 1984). Meisels and Atkins-Burnett (1994) summarize the limitations of developmental screening tests the following way: Data from developmental screening should only be viewed as preliminary information regarding children's development; diagnostic or assessment decisions should not be made using screening instruments alone.

There are a number of misuses that should be avoided when using the results of screening tests. These include using screening information to make decisions regarding school entrance, using the score on a developmental screening tests as an IQ score, or labeling children based upon their score on a screening test. Meisels also cautions that screening instruments should not be used with populations to which they are not sensitive (e.g., culturally, linguistically, or socioeconomically different children). In addition, developmental screening should not be done outside of the educational context, one in which assessment, evaluation, and intervention takes place.

In the appendix, examples of developmental screening tests are described. These descriptions include what is covered in the test as well as who is qualified to administer the test.

Diagnostic Tests

A diagnostic test is used to identify the existence of a disability or specific area of academic weakness in a child. Test results are used to suggest possible causes for the disability or academic weakness as well as to suggest potential remediation strategies.

Unlike many developmental screening or readiness tests, diagnostic tests are usually administered by highly trained individuals such as school and clinical psychologists, speech pathologists, social workers, guidance counselors, and teachers. Frequently, a child who is undergoing diagnostic assessment may be seen by a group of professionals known as a multidisciplinary assessment team.

As stated earlier, developmental screening should not be used for diagnostic purposes. While many of the same types of behaviors are assessed by both instruments, screening devices are very limited and brief, while diagnostic instruments have a much more comprehensive scope.

Some diagnostic instruments may be specialized and used when a specific learning problem is indicated. For example, if a child has language that is unintelligible, what might be warranted is a diagnostic articulation test. If the child has intelligible speech, but has poor conceptual or other general language difficulties, a different type of language assessment might be called for. If, on the other hand, the child demonstrates general cognitive delays, an IQ test or other measure of cognitive abilities may be warranted.

In the appendix, a number of diagnostic instruments are listed and described. As will be seen, the scope of the tests varies as do the ages of the children that they are intended for. Some of the instruments are very specialized by developmental domain while some are general. Some are specialized by specific age range while others are appropriate for early childhood through adulthood.

Readiness Tests

Readiness tests are used in early childhood education to assess the degree to which children are prepared for an academic or preacademic program (NAEYC, 1988a). They are similar in form and content to achievement tests in that they measure children's mastery over specific curriculum content. However, readiness tests do not assess this to the extent that an achievement test would, in either depth or breadth. Achievement tests are used primarily to determine children's mastery over curriculum content after a period of instruction, while readiness tests assess what content children have mastered in order to determine how "ready" they are to go on to the next phase of instruction. Most readiness tests are criterion referenced and have items that focus on general knowledge and skill achievement and performance (Meisels, 1987).

According to Meisels (1987), many people confuse readiness tests with developmental screening tests. They are similar in that both are brief and are used as a sorting device to some extent. However, Meisels points out that the purpose of the two is very different. As stated earlier, the purpose of a developmental screening test is to sort out those children who may be in need of further diagnostic testing in order to determine if they require special education services. The purpose of a readiness test is to determine the specific skills and knowledge children have mastered. The results of readiness tests are used for both placement and curriculum planning. As such, readiness tests are product oriented—measuring the skills and knowledge the child already possesses—while developmental screening tests are process oriented—measuring the child's ability to acquire new knowledge and skills.

Because readiness tests do not directly measure children's potential for future learning, they do not adequately predict future academic achievement (Wiske, Meisels, & Tivnan, 1981). Simply stated, readiness tests cannot validly be used to predict future academic success in children. Instead, they describe children's current level of academic knowledge and skills. The issue of school readiness is discussed further in Chapter 6.

A number of readiness and achievement tests commonly used in early childhood education are described in the appendix. As will be noted, many are group tests and are administered by the classroom teacher or trained paraprofessional. The intended use of each of the specific tests along with a description of what is assessed by the instruments is included.

Achievement Tests

Many early childhood programs use achievement tests to assess children's progress or level of attainment. An achievement test measures the extent to which an individual has achieved certain information or attained skills that are identified within curricular objectives (Wortham, 2001). Assessments can only be beneficial for educational planning and curriculum modification if the assessment is linked to the curriculum content and method of instruction. If this condition is met, then various forms of standardized assessments can be used for planning instruction, reporting children's progress, and evaluating the effectiveness of the educational experience. Issues related to these purposes for assessment are discussed in Chapter 2.

Related to assessment for educational planning and curriculum planning is the timing of assessment. While it has been suggested earlier that assessment should be ongoing and occur throughout the school year, there are specific times when assessment may be useful for different purposes (Wortham, 2001).

Children are assessed at the beginning of the school year in order for teachers to better understand the individual differences that occur among children. In addition, assessment at the beginning of the school year also gives teachers information related to a child's current level of developmental and educational functioning. Assessment at the beginning of the year is the place from which to start and may suggest to the teacher ways to design learning activities for individual children or the class in general.

While assessing children at the beginning of the year provides a starting place, it must be kept in mind that children should be assessed continuously throughout the year. This information is useful for planning and modification of the curriculum.

Children should also be assessed at the end of a learning unit or at the end of the reporting period. The timing of this assessment is useful for developing a clearer understanding of children's progress in the curriculum. It also provides useful information for teachers in describing children's learning to families. If standardized assessments are used, it is important to remember that translating the findings into behavioral terms with examples is most useful for families to understand. For most families, scores don't mean anything and often will result in families asking comparative questions about their child that may be inappropriate or unproductive.

Another time at which assessment should take place is at the end of the school year. This is an important time to assess children to determine the progress the child has made during the school year in order to report this information to the next teacher and to families. At the end of the school year, assessment is more comprehensive and usually includes assessing children's performance in all areas of the curriculum. In some cases this may include standardized achievement tests as well as teacher-made tests or other forms of assessment.

According to Aschbacher (2000), a school or school district planning to use achievement tests should:

- Know the limitations of achievement testing, particularly for young children.
- Become aware of the new types of achievement tests that emphasize problem solving and have items with multiple correct responses, rather than just having one right response to each item.
- Recognize that not until about third grade do children have the reading and writing skills and capacity to remember detail required by achievement tests; therefore, testing should start no earlier than third grade.
- Have the teachers prepare the children in advance for taking the test by identifying appropriate test-taking strategies. These can include specific ways to follow directions, working within a time frame, and marking answers in the same way that the test requires.

USING THE APPROPRIATE MEASURE

Four types of standardized assessments have been described above. It is important to understand that these assessments are not interchangeable and their use is determined by why it is that you want to assess a child.

The *Standards for Educational and Psychological Testing* (AERA, APA, & NCME, 1999) offers suggestions on what kinds of things to consider when choosing the appropriate assessment. These suggestions help you consider the purpose of the test based on a number of factors including the child's age and developmental level, ethnicity, language background, logistical considerations, and the psychometric properties of the assessment (Mindes, 2003). Consider the following questions when determining the appropriateness of an assessment instrument:

- When was the assessment developed and normed?
- How long will it take to administer the test?
- What is the appropriate age range for which the test was developed?
- Who is qualified to administer the assessment?
- What is the general purpose of the test?
- Is the assessment standardized?
- Are there multiple purposes for which the assessment can be used reliably?
- What specific behavior or knowledge is assessed?
- Does the test have subtests, and are they related to each other?
- Is the assessment available in multiple languages?

- Are the directions for administration clear?
- How complicated is it to administer to children?
- Is special training or certification required to administer the test?
- What kind of scores does the assessment yield?
- Are there suggestions in the testing manual for reporting the findings in a clear and meaningful way to families?
- Do the test results help parents and teachers have a clearer understanding of the child as learner?

In this chapter, various types of formal assessments were described. They included developmental screening tests, diagnostic tests, readiness tests, and achievement tests. Suggestions for considering which type of test to use were also presented. In Chapter 5, specific characteristics of formal assessment instruments and the terminology associated with them will be discussed. The understanding of these concepts will make the user and interpreter of assessment outcomes better prepared to make choices and decisions regarding children and curriculum.

Characteristics and Uses of Standardized Test Results

MEASUREMENT HAS been defined as "the process of determining, through observation or testing, an individual's traits or behaviors, a program's characteristics, or the property of some other entity, and then assignment of a number, rating, or score to that determination" (Goodwin & Goodwin, 1982, p. 523). It is important for early childhood practitioners to be familiar with measurement terminology in order to be good consumers of and users of test results. This knowledge will help an early childhood practitioner understand:

- How to evaluate the worthiness of a particular test
- How better to use the results of a test
- How to make better use of other types of assessments (Mindes, 2003)

According to the National Association for the Education of Young Children (1988b), "teachers are responsible for administering tests and, therefore, have a professional responsibility to be knowledgeable about appropriate testing and to influence, or attempt to influence, the selection and use of tests" (p. 43).

This chapter will discuss the terminology associated with a standardized test score itself, and the terms associated with how the scores are derived and subsequently the meaning of those scores for practical purposes. The intent in this chapter is to convey a general understanding of the deviation of a score and how that score relates to other scores, as well as an understanding of the nature of the test and its derived score.

TERMINOLOGY

There are a number of terms that are used in assessment, some of which are used with both standardized tests and tests that have no standardization (i.e., teacher-made tests), and others which are used exclusively with standardized assessments.

Raw Scores

The *raw score* is probably the easiest term to understand as it represents the actual score that an individual attains on a given assessment measure, usually the number of items answered correctly. Raw scores are obtained on both published standardized measures as well as on teacher-made tests. In and of themselves, raw scores have little significance to educators for comparing one score to another or making curricular decisions based upon them. The primary reason for this is that raw scores from different measures do not emanate from the same referent.

For example, if an assessment has 25 items and a child achieves a raw score of 20 (20 items correct) and later receives a raw score of 20 on an assessment that consists of 35 items, these two raw scores do not mean the same thing. Conversely, if one child scored 20 on a test with 25 items and another child scores 10, it doesn't mean that the first child did twice as well on the test as the second child. In order for these scores to be comparable in any sense of the word, they need to become standardized in some way so that they have comparable meaning. One of the most useful ways for early childhood practitioners to begin the standardization process is to derive a measure of central tendency, using the raw scores.

Measures of Central Tendency

According to Goodwin and Goodwin (1996), "measures of central tendency provide summary numbers that inform us about the 'typical' score in a set of data" (p. 93). There are three different types of measures of central tendency.

Mean. The mean is nothing more than the arithmetic average of a group of scores: It is computed by summing all of the scores in the group of scores and dividing by the number of scores in the group. The mean may also be called the *average*. The mean is the most powerful of the measures of central tendency in that it takes into account all of the scores that are in the group. Everyone's score plays a part in the computation of the mean. It is important to know, however, that a mean may be skewed if there are a few scores that are *extreme outliers,* that is, that are discernibly higher or lower than most of the other scores. The mean is useful for indicating the average performance of a group on a measure, or the average performance of an individual on a number of measures over time (provided that the measures yield comparable raw scores).

Median. The median score represents the score in the middle of a distribution of scores. In order to compute the median, it is required that the scores in the group of scores be ordered from lowest to highest or highest to lowest. The score that is in the physical center of the distribution is the median score. For example, in the scores, 95, 94, 89, 87, 84, 81, 80, 78, 75, 74, 72, the median score is 81. Eighty-one is the score in the middle; there are five that are higher and five that are lower. If there are an even number of scores, the two middle scores are averaged and this then becomes the median. The median can also be thought of as the 50th percentile. The median is less sensitive to highly skewed scores and therefore is a better measure of central tendency for scores that are highly skewed.

Mode. The mode represents the most frequently occurring score in a distribution of scores. In order to derive the mode, the number of times a particular score appears in a data set is counted. The score that appears most frequently is the mode. The advantage of using the mode is that its meaning is obvious; it represents the score that occurs most frequently. The disadvantage in using the mode is that many distributions have more than one mode. It is not recommended that the mode be the only measure of central tendency used.

Measures of Variability

Measures of variability indicate how disperse the distribution of scores is within a data set (Goodwin & Goodwin, 1996): the larger the difference among scores, the greater the variability. Conversely, variability will be less if the scores are tightly grouped together. The range and the standard deviation are two measures of variability that are commonly cited.

Range. The range is a rudimentary measure of variability. The range is calculated by determining the difference between the highest score in the distribution and the lowest. It is not a very sensitive measure in that it only takes into account two scores, the lowest and the highest. It is simply an indication of the difference between the highest and lowest scores in a data set.

The difficulty with all of the statistics that have been discussed thus far is that unlike scores from two sources cannot be compared. For example, if a child scores a 42 on a test of cognitive development and an 18 on a language assessment, it is not possible to discern if these scores are comparable or different from each other using a measure of central tendency or the range. In order to compare them, they must be converted to a standard score.

Standard deviation. Simply stated, the standard deviation is the average amount that a particular score is from the mean. The larger the standard deviation is, the greater the spread of the scores in that distribution is from the mean. Conversely, the smaller the standard deviation, the more homogeneous the scores are, indicating that there is not much deviation among them. While the calculation of the standard deviation is beyond the scope of this book, it is important to know what it means and how to use it.

In the example given above, the individual's scores on a cognitive measure and a language measure can be compared using the standard deviation. Assume that the mean score on the cognitive assessment is 40 and the standard deviation is 1.50, and that the mean score on the language assessment is 20 and the standard deviation is 0.75. If the child's score is 42 on the cognitive assessment, this individual's score is 1.50 standard deviations above the mean. This same child scored 18 on a language assessment that had a mean of 20, which is about 0.66 standard deviations below the mean. This child's score on the cognitive assessment and the language assessment can now be compared. Because the score on the cognitive assessment is 1.50 standard deviations above the mean, and the score on the language assessment is 0.66 standard deviations below the mean, it can now be determined that the child scored better on the cognitive assessment than on the language assessment. This will provide useful information for getting a better understanding of the child's individual strengths for curriculum development.

There are far more statistics involved in the assessment process than have been described here. However, those that have been the focus of this chapter thus far are the essential ones to know in order to make sense out of the scores that are derived from standardized assessments. While the statistical elements of assessment are important, the actual characteristics of standardized assessments are also important in order to understand:

- How a test is developed
- What use is appropriate for the test
- What different types of scores are derived from different tests
- If a test is valid
- If a test is reliable
- If a test is practical

These are the focus of the discussion that follows.

STANDARDIZED REFERENCES FOR TESTS

Designers of standardized tests must consider certain characteristics when developing the measures. One of the primary characteristics considered is the standard reference to which children will be compared. In this section, two such standard references will be discussed.

Norm-Referenced Tests

Norm-referenced tests "have norms, sets of scores obtained from one or more samples of respondents" (Goodwin & Goodwin, 1996, p. 83). Norm-referenced tests are used when one is interested in comparing a child's performance with those of a representative group of children (Boehm, 1992; Wortham, 1990). The children with whom the comparison is made may be of a similar age or grade level.

The primary use of norm-referenced tests is to make educational decisions for children related to selection and classification (Boehm, 1992). Most intelligence tests and achievement tests are examples of norm-referenced, standardized tests.

Cryan (1986) states that there are three principal reasons for using norm-referenced tests. First, they should be used to assess the individual on information that is not sequential and where no specific level of competency is essential for making educational determinations. Second, they should be used when there is a need to choose an individual from among a group because a norm-referenced test will give teachers information regarding a child's relative performance. Finally, a norm-referenced test is used when it becomes imperative to examine individual differences. Because the scores are standardized according to a norming sample, they provide an equal basis from which to compare individual scores.

The scores on a standardized norm-referenced test may be reported in a number of ways. Some of the more common methods of reporting scores are discussed below.

Standard scores. Standard scores permit the comparison of a child's performance on one test to his or her performance on another test. The standard score is derived statistically using the child's actual performance score and comparing it to the average score and theoretical range of scores to be expected for the population.

Percentile scores. Percentile scores indicate an individual child's ranking in the distribution of scores indicated by the comparison group. It indicates what percentage of the comparison group scored either above or below the target child's score. For example, if a child received a percentile score of 72, it would indicate that this particular child scored better than 72% of the children that he or she was being compared to and lower than 28%. Conversely, if a child's percentile ranking was 26, it would indicate that 74% of the children in the comparison group received higher scores.

Age-equivalent scores. An age-equivalent score indicates the average chronological age of children achieving a particular score on a test. If, for example, a child who has a chronological age of 5 years, 8 months receives a raw score on a test that translates into an age-equivalent score of 6 years, 2 months, it would mean that this score was 6 months above what would be expected for a child of his or her age.

Grade-equivalent scores. Grade-equivalent scores are closely related to age-equivalent scores except that the comparison is by grade level rather than by chronological age. Often the grade-equivalent score is reported in years and months. A grade-equivalent score of 2-6 means that the score attained would be one that would be expected from the average child in the sixth month of second grade. Comparisons among children can be made using grade-equivalent scores as is the case with age-equivalent scores.

Criterion-Referenced Tests

Unlike norm-referenced tests, criterion-referenced tests are not concerned with children's performance relative to a comparison group. Rather a criterion-referenced test measures the degree to which a child has attained a certain level of accomplishment according to a specified performance standard. Often, criterion-referenced tests are used to determine the effects of instruction, and performance standards can either be in the form of behavioral or instructional objectives.

Boehm (1992) discusses two major advantages to using criterion-referenced tests. First, this form of assessment is concerned with children's mastery over instructional skills, knowledge, or processes. It does not concern itself with the comparison of children. Second, the results of criterion-referenced tests more easily translate into instructional goals. Contrasted to a norm-referenced test, where the performance score does not indicate how the child achieved the score, the criterion-referenced test is specifically related to the child's performance on an instructional sequence. Therefore, individualizing instruction is facilitated.

Gronlund (1973) lists several standards against which criterion-referenced measures should be compared. These standards are detailed in Boehm (1992), and include criteria regarding the tasks measured, the sequential presentation of tasks, and the standards by which children are judged.

First, the tasks measured should be clearly defined. In doing so, the behavioral criteria that are to be used as evidence of having achieved a level of competence should be operationalized so that they can be reliably observed and measured. If it proves difficult to decide whether or not a child is exhibiting a particular behavior, then perhaps this criterion has not been met.

Second, a detailed task analysis description of the expected sequence of behaviors should be provided. This will be achieved using some type of categorical structure of behaviors. Behaviors may be grouped sequentially under such headings as fine motor skills, problem-solving skills, communication skills, or social skills. It should also be noted whether or not an adequate sampling of behaviors under each of the skill areas has been used.

Third, the standards by which children are rated should be clearly stated. As such, the criterion levels that indicate "success" should be specifically outlined. In this manner, the results of the scored assessment should describe the child's behaviors clearly.

According to Cryan (1986), there are a number of conditions to consider when making the decision to use criterion-referenced tests. Criterion-referenced tests should be used when the following conditions exist:

1. Educators are interested in locating specific areas of difficulty that children are having related to curricular performance. This might include locating strengths as well as weaknesses.
2. Educators are trying to determine proficiency or competency levels in children. This would be important to ascertain when determining their next level of instruction.
3. The skills or processes that make up the subject being taught are sequenced. Sequencing may represent increasing levels of complexity (such as the steps necessary to solve problems requiring different mathematical operations) or simple ordering or quantifiable sequencing (such as the necessity to learn the names of many different shapes and/or colors before more complex processes can be attained).

PSYCHOMETRIC CHARACTERISTICS OF STANDARDIZED MEASURES

In order to determine whether or not a particular standardized measure will be useful for a particular educational situation, there are a number of psychometric properties of the instrument that should be considered. In this section, a number of these properties, along with their implications, will be discussed.

Test Validity

Test validity is the degree to which an instrument assesses what it purports to assess. It is important to know about an assessment instrument's validity in order to determine how useful the information taken from the test will be in making inferences. There are a number of different types of validity that may be reported in the test manual.

Content validity. Content validity refers to the extent to which the test's content is related to the intended purpose of the test. For example, in a reading readiness achievement test used in early childhood education, the content would be the curriculum content, instructional strategies, and curriculum and instruction goals. By providing information on content validity, test developers are defining the extent to which items in the test assess the objectives outlined in the test, thus fulfilling the purpose of the test (Wortham, 1990).

Knowledgeable assessment consumers should likewise determine the extent to which the expressed objectives and the purpose of the test matches their curriculum content, instructional strategies, and overall goals.

Criterion-related validity. Criterion-related validity provides evidence that the resulting scores on a particular assessment instrument are related to one or more outcome criteria. Two types of criterion-related validity are usually reported.

The first type is called *concurrent validity*. Concurrent validity refers to the degree the score on a test is related to the score on a different but similar test. For example, children's scores on one achievement test may be compared with their scores on a different achievement test. If the children's scores on the two tests are highly correlated, then they may be used as evidence of concurrent validity.

The second type of criterion-related validity is called *predictive validity*. The concern of predictive validity is with stability of the test score over time. It was reported earlier in this book that some developmental screening instruments do not have good predictive validity. That is, they may present a satisfactory measure of children's current development, but they do not accurately predict their future status. If a test has good predictive validity, it can be used as an indicator of future scores when related constructs are assessed.

Test Reliability

Reliability is a measure of test consistency. That is, it is an indication of how dependable and repeatable the score of a given test is. The higher the reliability coefficient, the greater likelihood that differences in an individual's scores over repeated test administrations is due to test-taker performance, rather than to test error of measurement. Three types of reliability can be reported.

Test-retest reliability. In test-retest reliability, a single form of a test is administered to a norming or experimental group for the purpose of establishing reliability. After a short interval of time the test is readministered to the same group, and the scores from the first administration are compared (using correlational analysis) with the second set of scores. The correlation coefficient will be an indication of how closely the scores from both administrations are related. If the correlation is high and positive, it is an indication that the test was consistent in measuring its objectives.

Split-half reliability. In split-half reliability, the norming or experimental group is administered the test for which reliability is to be established. The scores on one half of the test are compared (using correlational analysis) with the scores on the second half of the test. If the correlation coefficient is high and positive, this is an indication that the test is internally consistent in measuring the same objectives.

Alternate-form reliability. There are situations when it is appropriate to have two different forms of a test, with both forms designed to measure the same characteristics. The Peabody Picture Vocabulary Test and the Metropolitan Readiness Test are two examples of tests that have alternate forms. It may be important to have alternate forms of a test if it becomes necessary to administer a given test to the same group of children during a very short period of time. If you administer the exact same form of the test, confounding variables, such as familiarity with the content or a practice effect, may influence the scores. In alternate-form reliability the two alternate forms of the test are administered to a single group of children. The second form of the test is administered after a short interval of time. The scores on the first form of the test are then compared with the scores on the second form of the test in much the same manner as in the other two types of reliability described above. A test with high positive alternate-form reliability is an indication that both forms can be used interchangeably.

Assessment Practicality

Although validity and reliability are important psychometric qualities of assessment instruments that should be considered when selecting a test, the assessment tool's practicality must also be considered. This is the degree to which the teacher or others can utilize the information derived from the assessment instrument to make decisions about children or curriculum and instruction. There are two questions to consider when deciding on the practicality of the assessment.

First, how well do the objectives of the test match the objectives of the curriculum and instructional strategies used in the early education setting? Just as it is foolish to use a hearing test to determine visual acuity, so it is foolish to use an assessment instrument that is not related to the curriculum that the children are participating in. If the curriculum and assessment are not closely related, analysis of the test outcome will do little to help teachers use the results of the analyses for curriculum development or modification.

Second, how well does the test (content and procedures) match the developmental characteristics of the children for whom it was intended? The issue here is how valid and reliable a test is in its relation to the developmental stage of the child. That is, it is generally true that because young children are not good test takers, the younger the child is, the less likely it is that the test will be reliable and valid. This factor must be considered when choosing tests and interpreting test results. Chapter 3 details the developmental characteristics of children that must be considered when making decisions about testing.

NAEYC (2003) also relates the lack of reliability and validity in tests designed for young children to the rapid rate at which these children develop. This necessitates assessment administrations both often and in different contexts if accurate and up-to-date information is to be available for decision making. Cryan (1986) and Shepard and Smith (1986) point out that when this issue is not considered, the result is inappropriate placement of children and detrimental labeling.

USING STANDARDIZED TEST RESULTS

Using the results of standardized tests must be put into perspective. There are many ways to use them and many ways in which they should not be used. What is important to remember is that the standardized test score is only one source of information that can be reported. In this section, two appropriate ways to use standardized test results will be discussed: reporting standardized test results to families and using standardized test results for program accountability.

Reporting to Families

It should be remembered that a standardized test score is nothing more than a snapshot of a child's ability. It represents just one moment in time and represents only one aspect of the child's performance. This is especially true in early childhood education, where test performance is not always valid and reliable.

If standardized tests are used in the classroom, it is the parents' right to know the results of their child's performance on any given assessment measure. According to Wortham (1990), parents should be given their child's standardized test score so that they have a better understanding of the following:

1. Their child's performance as compared to the national norms that are established for that test
2. Their child's progress in the classroom as compared to other children who are in the same grade
3. Their child's strengths and needs regarding individual curriculum objectives

Simply providing the parents with a test score can be confusing to them. It is the responsibility of the teacher to explain the meaning of the score. What is important here is that the teacher also provide descriptions of actual classroom behaviors to go along with the test score so that the parents have a better understanding of the meaning and implication of their child's score. It would also be helpful to provide the parents with examples of actual classroom work that would also amplify the meaning of the score. In that manner, the parents will have the opportunity to see through example how the score may or may not translate into classroom work.

A danger in this is if the teacher only provides the parents with the test score and not its meaning or interpretation. This is especially true if the test score does not accurately reflect the child's level of accomplishment in the daily classroom work. There are many children who are not good test takers, and there are many tests that do not fit the child's way of thinking or performing. To repeat an earlier idea, it is important to relate to the parents that the test score is only one element in the equation of academic success.

Another important aspect of reporting the findings of test scores to parents is that the teacher explain how the test score will be used for future curriculum planning for their child. Nothing is more disheartening for a parent than to feel that the test score is a life sentence from which the child will never escape. This is especially true when the test score is below that which the parent or the teacher feels reflects adequate performance. Therefore it is imperative that the teacher explain how test scores are used by the school for the purpose of improving the academic experience for the child.

Finally, because the test score only reflects a moment in time, it is important for the teacher to put that score into perspective and also talk to the parents about their child's progress. While any particular test score may not be what would be considered "on grade level" or at the appropriate developmental level for the child's age, if the child is progressing in achievement over time, this should also be an important element of what is discussed with the parents.

Testing and Accountability

Only 3 days after taking office in 2001, President Bush proposed the No Child Left Behind Act (NCLB). Less than a year later the NCLB Act became the keystone of what would become sweeping education reform based on achieving the educational goals of accountability, choice, and flexibility (U.S. Department of Education, 2002b). Child assessment and program standards became the means by which these goals were to be accomplished. The NCLB Act mandated that all children in Grades 3–8 be tested annually in order to ensure that they reach proficiency by the 12th grade. As stated earlier, the act also led to some states testing children before Grade 3.

As stated previously, one of the immediate outcomes of this act was that every state developed standards for performance and content (Align to Achieve, 2003). What followed was that states began aligning curriculum frameworks to the state's standards (Scott-Little et al., 2003).

According to the NCLB Act fact sheet (U.S. Department of Education, 2002a), testing works. The fact sheet describes three reasons why testing will work to meet the goals of the act.

Testing provides information. The NCLB Act contends that children can't be helped to improve until teachers and families understand what children can do and what they understand. According to the act, assessment will raise the expectations for all children and ensure no slippage for any child. This will be accomplished by the following:

- Every state setting standards that are explicit and high for what children at each grade level should know and be able to do
- States measuring each child according to those standards by assessing them with tests that are aligned with the standards

The fact sheet points out that testing is not a new phenomenon and claims that teachers and school districts have always used tests to measure how children are performing.

Testing measures children's progress. Measuring children's progress on a regular basis will lead to these outcomes:

- Good instruction will ensure that all children will make substantial progress academically, every year and in every class.
- Parents and teachers will know that children are making progress toward meeting academic standards.
- Principals will know precisely how much progress is being made by all children so that they, along with teachers, can make appropriate decisions about teacher inservice requirements and curriculum.
- Accountability information will be provided so that it can be used for the identification of strengths and weaknesses in the system.

Every child will be assessed. The NCLB Act mandates that every child in Grades 3–8 be assessed for the purpose of giving families "report cards" regarding the performance of their child's school. The provision of school accountability reports will be accomplished by the following:

- Breaking test scores down into categories that include economic background, race, and ethnicity. In this manner, teachers and families will better understand the academic progress of each group so that "no child will be left behind."
- Requiring that all schools be held accountable for making sure that all children learn at appropriate rates.
- Communicating to families, communities, policy makers, school boards, and schools in a clear and precise manner and in a format that is understandable to all, which schools are doing well and which schools are in need of improvement.

Although a good assessment system will do much toward making sure that children are making academic progress, that schools are making progress toward meeting curriculum standards, and that curriculum modifications are being made in an informed manner, educators need to avoid the pitfall of focusing on the test scores alone. We *must* make sure that "Leave No Child Behind" doesn't turn out to be "Leave No Score Behind."

As users of tests and test results, teachers and others working in early education settings must become informed consumers of early childhood assessment instruments and findings. When they are not, potential dangers exist. Knowing which type of standardized measure to use and understanding its psychometric properties represents only part of what one should consider. Chapter 6 discusses the range of factors to take into account in making informed decisions regarding early assessment.

Advantages and Disadvantages of Standardized Testing

STANDARDIZED ASSESSMENTS can provide valuable information about children's development, learning, and progress. The manner in which standardized assessments can provide this information and the purposes of standardized assessments have been discussed in the previous chapter. Using standardized test results can have consequences for children, teachers, and curriculum and instruction. These consequences can be either positive or negative depending on how these results are used. This chapter considers the advantages, as well as the disadvantages, of using standardized assessments.

ADVANTAGES OF STANDARDIZED ASSESSMENTS

Standard Administration

Standardized tests have standardized administration procedures. This is important in that it ensures that all children, regardless of where they are from or what their background may be, will receive the exact same instructions when given the test. In addition, the same amount of time is usually given to each child, and specific, objective scoring procedures are used. In this way, standard administration makes it easier to compare the results of the assessment across various children or from one test time to the next with a specific child.

Numerical Scores

Because standardized tests yield numerical scores, the results of the test are quantifiable. Quantifiable scores, usually in the form of raw scores can be statistically transformed into standard scores or norms. Again, this facilitates comparing a child's performance to that of other children of the same age or to the same child's previous performance if the assessment is administered more than once over time. Moreover, when raw scores are converted to standard scores, it makes it possible to compare a child's scores on different types of tests. Standard scores also make interpretation of the score more useful for developing teaching strategies or learning environments that may be beneficial to the child.

Norms

Most standardized assessment scores are norm referenced. As explained in Chapter 5, this means that the test has determined, on the average, what score children of a comparison group should achieve, and how deviations— either up or down from the average—can be interpreted. Again, this is very useful for comparing a child's scores to national averages, state averages, local averages, or classroom averages. This is an advantage as long as what is done with the results is appropriate and beneficial to the child.

Valid Results

Unlike more informal types of assessments, validity can be measured in standardized tests. As noted in Chapter 5, validity ensures that the test measures the characteristics of the child it purports to assess. Standardized assessments usually report a measure of validity within the test manual.

Reliable Results

Standardized assessments also are able to provide a measure of reliability (see Chapter 5), unlike other less formal types of assessment measures. It is important to know that if the child were given the test at a different time or in a different situation, the results would be the same. It is a measure of confidence in the assessment that the child's score will be consistent. Again, this is important for reporting to others how the child is performing in whatever area the test measures.

It should be noted that the advantages discussed here are only advantages if used within the scope of the intended purpose of the assessment. This aspect will be discussed more fully later in this chapter.

CRITICISMS OF STANDARDIZED
NORM-REFERENCED ASSESSMENTS

While there is a place for using norm-referenced assessments, they should not be the sole means of assessing children in the early childhood classroom. As long as the limitations of norm-referenced assessments are acknowledged, their results can be used in proper perspective. Some of these limitations are discussed below.

Administration

Standard test administration can be a benefit of standardized testing, but it can also be a detriment. As discussed in Chapter 3, children in the early childhood classroom represent vast differences in developmental levels, prior experiences, approaches to learning, motivation, and individual needs. Due to the nature of norm-referenced assessments, the instructions for test administration must be strictly followed. The same procedures are utilized for all children, and there is little room for modification of those procedures to meet special needs of individual children (Bagnato, Neisworth, & Munson, 1989).

Bias

The composition of the sample on which the norm-referenced assessment was standardized must be taken into consideration. Often the assessment is biased against children of different cultural or linguistic backgrounds or against children with developmental delays or special needs (Galagan, 1985; Tindal & Marston, 1986; Webster, McInnis, & Carver, 1986). These issues will be directly addressed in Chapters 10 and 11.

Influence on the Curriculum

Norm-referenced assessments do not reflect curriculum sensitivity (Airasian & Madaus, 1983; Cohen & Spenciner, 1994; Fuchs & Deno, 1981; Tindal & Marston, 1986). Many published norm-referenced assessments do not take into account contemporary approaches to curriculum and instruction in early childhood education. They are often based on skill development approaches and reflect a theoretical perspective that is more behavioral than constructivist. They assess specific skills or knowledge learned rather than the process of learning. This often leads to teachers teaching to the test, and thus the norm-referenced assessment has the effect of narrowing the curriculum. This is of particular concern given the passing of the No Child Left Behind Act of 2001 (U.S. Department of

Education, 2002b). This issue will be discussed more fully later in this chapter.

TESTING AND SCHOOL READINESS

According to the National Association for the Education of Young Children (Bredekamp, 1987) and others (Saluja, Scott-Little, & Clifford, 2000; Shore, 1998), ongoing assessment and evaluation in early childhood education occurs primarily to determine children's curricular needs. Some educators, however, advocate that certain types of assessment and evaluation may be used for purposes other than this (e.g., Uphoff & Gilmore, 1986), particularly for children about to enter kindergarten. They propose that children be assessed to determine whether or not they are "ready" for school. A central assumption of this position is that children should be homogeneously grouped in school according to developmental level rather than chronological age. Thus, if a child is of legal entry age for kindergarten, but tests at a younger developmental age, the child should be given the "gift of time"—or another year—to become ready for the curriculum. Readiness is central to this issue, yet there are many interpretations of the underlying constructs defining readiness.

Readiness is a term often associated with early childhood education. Its use, however, is not standardized. The concept is often used to describe how prepared children are to "formal schooling," "formal reading instruction," or "formal math instruction," or to move on to the next grade level. In this regard, one interpretation of the readiness concept utilizes assessment to determine whether or not children are ready for a particular experience. If through assessment it is determined that children are not ready, it may preclude them from participating in some experiences, or from starting kindergarten altogether.

In another interpretation of readiness, children are assessed to determine what experiences they are ready to encounter. This interpretation is consistent with principles of developmentally appropriate practice in that it would not prohibit children from participating in any educational experiences, but would suggest what and how educational experiences should be modified to meet children's developmental needs. This latter interpretation of the readiness concept is also more consistent with current knowledge of child development in that readiness is determined by the individual child's development, and it is known that in the early years children do not develop at the same rate and that their development is in constant flux.

Because children do not develop at the same rate and the development of young children is in constant and rapid flux, important implications regarding assessment and readiness are apparent. While children are in prekindergarten, kindergarten, and first grade, teachers should expect differences in academic performance among children because of differences in their rates of development. Theoretically, by the time these children reach third grade the expectation would be that many of these differences would have disappeared—that is, if one holds with the current tenets concerning child development. However, in practice, this usually will not occur. Most of the time, these early differences will not have disappeared. It is possible that teacher assessments of pupils in lower grades have caused the teacher to treat those children who were slower to develop differently than those who developed at a faster rate, inadvertently reinforcing developmental differences and solidifying student status.

Another problem educators must be aware of is that the practice of testing to determine developmental level for purposes of school readiness and entrance may constitute both a class and a gender bias. Children who come from homes of economic poverty and boys, in general, will be overidentified by developmental readiness instruments as those not ready for school. Both socioeconomic status (SES) and gender have been shown to correlate with scores on tests such as these (Shepard & Smith, 1988).

According to Piaget (Inhelder, Sinclair, & Bovet, 1974), children's construction of knowledge and problem-solving abilities—two processes assessed in tests used for the purposes described above—are the manifestation of the interaction among the developmental factors of maturation, physical and social experience, and equilibration. Although maturation is biologically determined, the remaining two factors are not. Therefore, a child's score on a developmental readiness test is only partially the result of the maturational process. Still, those who advocate using readiness tests to determine if children are ready for school maintain that maturation alone—or time—is sufficient to bolster children's developmental level and knowledge sufficiently to prepare them for the kindergarten experience.

Much of the variance in readiness test scores among groups of children is due to the types of self-selected or societally selected experiences that each child has had, not from differences in level of maturity. Thus the belief of gift-of-time advocates that they are segregating out children who lack the appropriate maturational level necessary for success in early schooling is erroneous. What they are segregating out are those who have not had the appropriate physical and social experiences that most kindergarten curricula require as measures of success—and in all likelihood, the kindergarten class may be the only place where these children can receive these experiences.

Assessment instruments such as those used to determine school readiness in children examine development as though it can be photographed and scrutinized at one frozen moment in time. In essence, the assessment ignores the child's past physical and social experiences that have influenced the responses. In addition, it cannot determine what type of experiences the child may require in the future, or how the child will benefit from those experiences.

Schooling decisions based upon readiness testing take various forms. One is to prohibit children's entrance into kindergarten for an additional year. Another is to place children into what has come to be called a "developmental kindergarten," which is the 1st year of a 2-year kindergarten track; these children will thus spend 2 years in kindergarten before being promoted to first grade. Still another is to place children in a "transitional first grade" after kindergarten. In this format, children identified as "not ready" will spend 2 years in first grade before being passed into second. Both of these forms of early childhood "retention" are discussed in the next section.

The schooling practice most often associated with readiness testing is the delaying of children's entrance into kindergarten for an additional year. As was mentioned earlier, this practice represents a classist and sexist bias and has the potential for impeding the development of those children who are most in need of the experiences they will miss by not being in school. This is particularly true for children from economic poverty and others who come from environments that do not afford them the types of experiences they require for even modest success in today's schools.

Cognitive development, however, is not only the product of maturation but also the result of the interplay of maturation with physical and social experiences. Children from economic poverty who are kept out of school for an additional year will probably not undergo the kinds of experiences they need to prepare them for school. On the other hand, middle-SES children denied entrance to kindergarten are much more likely to encounter the kinds of enriching experiences they need before entering school. Thus, by keeping both these children out of school, the developmental gap between children from environments of relative advantage and disadvantage is likely to widen even more.

Rather than a "ready" child, educators should be thinking in terms of a "ready" school. This concept implies that it is the responsibility of a school to be ready for all children whether or not they are identified as "ready" to learn according to some external standard (Shore, 1998). Because age is the criterion for kindergarten entrance, the implication is that the states must also consider having "ready" schools as their policy (Maxwell & Clifford, 2004); unfortunately, this is not their practice.

DELETERIOUS EFFECTS ASSOCIATED WITH THE PRACTICE OF TESTING

In a discussion of the advantages and disadvantages of standardized testing, it must be emphasized that the application of the assessment findings is what will ultimately determine whether the advantage is truly an advantage or a disadvantage is a truly a disadvantage. There are a number of deleterious effects that are associated with the practice of testing in early childhood education. These occur in all aspects of education, affecting the curriculum, the school organizations, and the children themselves.

Effects on Curriculum and Instruction

Overreliance on a test or test results could have an adverse affect on the curriculum. Teachers may inadvertently or deliberately teach to the test in order to increase the scores of the children in their class. This has the effect of narrowing the curriculum so that the learning of information tested by the test becomes the primary curriculum goal and objective. In addition, schools may look to tests to determine curricular goals and objectives, thereby relinquishing their duties of curriculum development to the test writers and publishers. Meisels (1989) labeled this practice *high-stakes testing*. High-stakes testing adversely affects the curriculum and subsequently the children.

A recent issue related to the high-stakes testing of young children and a potential misuse of the testing data is the proposed Head Start National Reporting System (NRS). The NRS has three stated purposes:

1. Enhance local collection and aggregation of both child outcome assessment data and local program evaluation.
2. Enhance the ability of the Head Start Bureau and the ACF Regional Offices to plan for technical training and assistance.
3. Use the data for future Head Start monitoring reviews.

Meisels and Atkins-Burnett (2004) criticize the NRS for using a high-stakes approach to assessment with 4-year-olds in Head Start. The implementation of the NRS will result in the largest number of young children being exposed to standardized achievement tests than ever before in this country's history. What is most troubling about this, according to Meisels and Atkins-Burnett, is that the NRS

includes items that are rife with class prejudice and are developmentally inappropriate. This is particularly troubling because the test is being used by Head Start officials as a quality assurance system. In fact, the idea that a narrow test of young children's skills in literacy and math can represent a quality indicator of a holistic program like Head Start shows a stunning lack of appreciation for the comprehensive goals of the . . . program. . . . program quality cannot be evaluated by student outcomes alone, since this approach does not take into account differences among children and programs. (p. 64)

As with other criticisms related to the high-stakes testing of young children, the design of the NRS has been shown to be inaccurate and the results are poor predictors of children's later achievement. Much of this has to do with the fact that the development of children at this age is in rapid flux, and this alone can lead to misleading results (Meisels & Atkins-Burnett, 2004). The feared outcome is an inevitable narrowing of the Head Start curriculum to ensure "adequate" testing results.

While one effect of high-stakes testing is to narrow the curriculum within an individual classroom, another harmful effect of testing associated with this curriculum practice is when assessment and evaluation entirely determines the program. This is referred to as "measurement-driven instruction" (Madaus, 1988; Mindes, 2003). Some school systems use test results for teacher and program accountability. In order to increase the likelihood of higher test scores, teachers will then often base their decisions about what to teach and how to teach it on what information and processes will be assessed by the end-of-the-year test. The effect of this is to narrow the curriculum to those topics that are covered by the test or are most subject to being measured by a test.

Meisels (1989) cautions that this practice often results in a curriculum and instruction style that is rigid and lacks creativity and imagination. It also has the effect of moving the curriculum away from being child centered to being content centered—that is, the content that is covered on the test. If instruction is measurement driven, the teacher is relinquishing responsibility for curriculum development to those who design the tests, in essence giving test publishers control over the school curriculum (Madaus, 1988). This practice may even determine the sequence in which curriculum content is taught.

I recall a kindergarten teacher, "Ms. Smith," with whom I taught during my first year in the public schools. At the end of each school year, a standardized test was administered to all kindergarten children for the purpose of planning the following year's instruction. Once it was known that each classroom's scores would be made available for examination by other teachers, parents, and other interested parties, the seriousness with which teachers entered into this annual ritual dramatically changed.

One year Ms. Smith was determined that her class would be at or near the top of the score distribution. She perused previous years' test results to determine what sorts of information were most troublesome to her students. She then focused her activities on the concepts and skills that she determined would have the biggest payoff for increasing test scores. Ms. Smith even moved her unit on Native Americans from autumn (Thanksgiving) to spring (closer to the actual time of testing) and planned a field trip to the local museum of natural history solely for the purpose of "teaching" her class what a moccasin was. No child in any of her previous classes had known what a moccasin was. She was determined that her children would get that item correct on the test this year. She was successful in making sure that all of her children now knew the concept *moccasin*, but talk about narrowing the curriculum!

While this story illustrates an extreme case, even minor infractions of this nature are antithetical to sound practice in early education that is grounded in developmental theory. What must be strived for is using tests to serve educational practice rather than determining it.

Effects on Children

Meisels (1987, 1989) contends that standardized test results are often misused and may lead to undesirable effects on both children and the curriculum. Some of the ways in which misuse of standardized test results affect children are:

1. Prohibiting children from entering a program due to their test performance even though they are legal entrance age
2. Placing children in inappropriate ability groupings
3. Using children's test performance on developmental screening instruments to predict their future academic performance

Inappropriate use of assessment information can have detrimental effects on children. One of the most costly errors that can occur is when testing leads to inappropriate labeling. As has been discussed earlier, young children are not reliable test takers. Again, a developmental rule applies here: the younger the children, the less reliable they are as test takers. One test that has come under scrutiny, the Gesell School Readiness Test, demonstrates that test results can lead to inappropriate labeling in young children (Meisels, 1987, 1989).

The Gesell School Readiness Test is administered to children prior to kindergarten entry in some school districts. The score that the children attain determines whether they are labeled "ready" or "not ready" to learn in kindergarten. It has been argued that the test may indicate what information the children have already learned, but not the extent to which, or the rate at which, new information can be learned. Thus tests may be able to paint a picture of what information has already been acquired by children, but test scores tell us little about children's rates of learning, modalities through which they learn, or the nature of their reasoning processes. Yet assumptions are made about children's cognitive processes on the basis of their score on a particular test.

Aside from resulting in inappropriate labeling of children, testing may also cause educators to view the nature of children's progress in fragmented and compartmentalized ways rather than in cohesive and integrative ways. While current trends in early childhood education are calling for curriculum practices that view progress as continuous and integrated, tests force artificial beginnings and ends of instructional sequences. This practice is simply used to facilitate the assessment of children's progress.

Many tests measure a restrictive range of learning and development, so understandings about children as the result of this kind of testing will be as narrow as the range of behaviors that are being assessed. There are at least two ways that tests reflect a narrow picture of children.

First, a test may be restrictive in the extent to which a particular skill or developmental domain is actually measured. When one thinks about the complexity of skills and processes involved in the development of language or cognition in children, it would be difficult to conceptualize an assessment instrument that could account for all of those complexities. While a particular test may be both reliable and valid, it is incumbent upon the user of the test to determine what it is that is actually being measured and not to interpret beyond that level.

Take, for example, a test of cognitive development, the results of which classify a child as being in one particular stage of cognitive development, say either preoperational or concrete operational. How does the test assesses this? What skills or processes does the test measure to make this determination? What skills does the test not measure? It is known that children may exhibit characteristics of being in more than one stage of cognitive development. This is known as *decalage*. If the children are not given the opportunity to demonstrate higher order skills and processes, we come away with a restrictive view of their developmental accomplishments. While a test like this may prove useful in certain situations, caution should be taken not to overextend the findings to contexts that are not applicable.

A second way a test may be restrictive in portraying children is when the social context that is reflected in the test content or procedures is discrepant from the one that the child is developing and learning in. Again, while this information may prove useful in a limited context, the question that must be asked is, what information do children have or what skills do they possess that are not being addressed in a particular test?

Inasmuch as tests, either standardized or teacher-made, are restrictive in the portrait that they paint, it is important not only to assess children's learning and development according to what tests can tell about them, but also to assess them in light of what the test is unable to reveal.

Effects on Professional Trends

Certain harmful educational practices in early childhood education have come to be associated with the practice of early-grade testing. Despite intended useful practices that can be associated with appropriate uses of test results, too often negative effects also result. The negative effects of testing in the early years impact more than just individual children or individual classrooms. These negative effects often manifest themselves on a district-wide basis.

Raising the mean age in class. Many states have school districts that require testing in prekindergarten. Many of these districts use these test results as guidelines for parents to make a decision about whether to send their child to school that year or wait an additional year. The result of this is that some children enter kindergarten at age 5, while others enter at age 6, even though they were of legal entry age at 5. The curricular trend that accompanies this practice is that in order to maintain the expectations at a level that accommodates the mean age in the class, requirements to perform in an "average" manner are raised to accommodate the older average age in the class. This makes it more difficult for the young 5s in the kindergarten to function in an average way because they are expected to act older than their actual age.

School systems have responded to this dilemma by systematically raising the legal entry age requirements. Shepard and Smith (1986) report that during the 1980s school districts gradually moved the entrance age for kindergarten higher. The effect of this is that the average age of children entering kindergarten has gotten older and older.

Today, the entrance age cutoff dates for kindergarten children are not uniform across the nation (Education Commission of the States, 2003). Following is a breakdown of the kindergarten entrance dates across the country:

- Six states have kindergarten cutoff dates between December 1 and January 1. The result is that these states will have a substantial mix of 4-year-olds and 5-year-olds in their kindergarten classes.
- Thirty-five states have kindergarten cutoff dates between August 31 and October 16. This will lead to fewer 4-year-olds in kindergarten, but still a substantial mix of 4- and 5-year-olds.
- Three states have kindergarten cutoff dates on or before August 15. These states will have a greater likelihood of having 5-year-olds in kindergarten.

- Six states leave the entrance-age cutoff question to the local school districts.

While the practice of raising the average age in class seems like an adjustment of sorts, the effect is that it changes the role and function of early education. In addition, it affects the expectations of what should occur prior to school entrance as well. As pointed out earlier, some children may be positively affected by such practices, many children, particularly those who reside in homes of economic poverty, may find themselves falling farther and farther behind. If this practice continues, the result may be separate educational systems, a condition some would say already exists.

Retention and transitional programs. When schools rely heavily on tests for placement of children, retention and transitional classes are two ways in which they deal with children they judge "unready" for a more "formal" curriculum. While transitional programs (2 years of kindergarten or 2 years of first grade) are thought to lessen the stigma associated with retention, they can be considered retention nonetheless. According to Shepard and Smith (1988), regardless of whether it takes 2 years to get to first grade or 3 years to get to second grade, all 2-year programs can be categorized as retention. Shepard and Smith list a number of retention euphemisms: prekindergarten, developmental kindergarten, buy-a-year, begindergarten, transitional first grade, readiness room, pre-first grade, and academic redshirting. The result is delaying school entry into first grade. Research has shown that delaying entrance into school, no matter how it's defined or what the form, is not beneficial to children (Marshall, 2003; Stipek, 2002).

While there is an intuitive conception that 2-year programs are beneficial for those children not considered ready for a traditional, more structured first-grade curriculum, research does not substantiate this contention. A number of studies that compared children who are in transition programs with children who were eligible for transition programs but did not attend, showed no differences in achievement performance levels (Gredler, 1984; Jones, 1985). In a later study, Shepard and Smith (1987) examined groups of children who were closely matched on age, sex, and readiness scores, and found that children who participated in transition programs received a mere one-month advantage on a number of variables when compared with children who went to schools whose systems did not participate in transition programs. These variables included reading levels, math performance, teachers' ratings of academic performance, self-concept, and attention.

While many studies seem to demonstrate that there are no realized benefits for children who participate in 2-year programs, some studies reveal that there could be detrimental effects. These negative effects fall into categories related to poor self-concept, negative attitudes toward school, feelings of failure, being bored, and being teased by peers (Bell, 1972; Shepard & Smith, 1985, 1987).

General Misuse of Testing Results

General misuse of testing results can create deleterious effects in any of the above categories (Maxwell & Clifford, 2004; Meisels & Atkins-Burnett, 2004; NAEYC, 2004). There are a number of ways in which test results can be misused. First, there may be an overuse of standardized tests. The concern over the overuse of standardized tests in early education is widespread (Wortham, 1990). Using standardized test results for teacher accountability, determining student participation in federally funded programs, comparing the quality of teaching among school districts, or as the basis upon which funding for schools is determined are all ways that have been cited as misuses of test results.

A second misuse, somewhat related to the first, is using standardized tests for a purpose not intended by the test developers. In one study, for example, Durkin (1987) found that teachers and administrators were using the Stanford Early Achievement Test (Madden, Gardner, & Collins, 1989) to determine which children should be promoted and which should go into a transitional class, in spite of the fact that the Stanford Early Achievement Test was designed to measure the progress of students.

Many times a test manual will give equivalent scores. The Peabody Picture Vocabulary Test—III (Dunn & Dunn, 1997), an assessment instrument designed to measure children's receptive vocabulary ability, gives IQ equivalent scores in the manual. Many mistakenly assume that this means that the test can interchangeably be used with an IQ test. It is important to remember to use the test results only as intended and described in the test manual.

A third misuse of standardized test results occurs when the test has been given to a population for which it was not intended (Santos, 2004). It is difficult to find a test that could be considered culture free, one that is not biased to give either an advantage or disadvantage to children of a particular cultural, racial, economic, ethnic, or linguistic group (see Chapter 11 for a more thorough discussion of this issue). The results of tests must therefore be interpreted with this in mind.

Finally, although standardized tests have established procedures, one cannot be assured that the tests are administered uniformly. Thus the results may be misused if they were inappropriately obtained. This can occur especially if they are group-administered tests given by a number of different classroom teachers. Testing young children proves even a greater challenge for group testing because difficulties related to attention, individual differences, fatigue, and distraction are exacerbated in group-administered early childhood standardized tests.

The preceding discussion of the problems that can arise in the administration of standardized tests and the misuse of their results is not exhaustive. The issues presented here are meant to serve as a structural guide for thinking about the problems and misuses of standardized tests. Further misuses of test information are discussed elsewhere in this book.

INHERENT DANGERS IN THE PRACTICE OF TESTING

Along with the practice of testing in early childhood education come inherent dangers that can result in the negative effects discussed above. Two of the most critical of these inherent dangers are human and environmental error factors associated with the testing and lack of acknowledging different rates and styles of learning in the children tested.

First, test administration as well as scores themselves are subject to both human and environmental error factors. As has been discussed earlier, young children are not good test takers. There are many developmental and environmental conditions that may affect test performance and subsequent scores. For example, young children are language bound. That is, they rely on the language of the test and administration directions to guide them through the procedures and lead them to making appropriate responses. Unfortunately, while the language of the test may be perfectly clear to those who develop the tests, young children often misinterpret what is expected of them, and this often leads to inappropriate responses.

Interpretations of test results are also subject to human error. Teachers seldom delve into an item analysis, and thus they rely on the total scores achieved by the children as indications of their performance levels.

Test scores are also subject to environmental factors. The configuration of items on a page, the number of items on a page, or the manner in which items are depicted are all factors that may affect children's performance. Again, the younger the children are, the more this is true. Often, standardized test formats alternate between presenting the sequence of items in a row and in a column. This may have disastrous effects on children who are used to one format or the other. If there are too many items on a page, it is not difficult for young children to lose their place or get out of sequence with no awareness that they have done this. Understanding that both human and environmental factors affect children's performances on tests may prove helpful in overcoming this danger, but even if the danger can't always be overcome, at least the importance of test outcomes can be put into perspective.

A second danger associated with the practice of testing in early child-hood education is that formal assessment measures seldom inform us about children's rates of learning, modes of learning, or their problem-solving abilities. As has been discussed in Chapter 3, young children's performances in early education settings can be stylized or can reflect individual charac-teristics of the child. These characteristics include varying rates of matura-tion, individual learning styles, and different approaches to solving problems. Unfortunately, tests are used within single formats and are meant to be appropriate for all children in a particular group. While the test may be able to provide information regarding what factual information children have (within the parameters of the test questions), tests are not individual enough to meet the developmental needs of each particular child.

Tests given at the conclusion of an instructional unit assume that all children require the same amount of time to process the information and acquire the knowledge or skills that unit addresses. This is a faulty assump-tion. Tests do not permit a divergence of problem-solving paths. Thus im-portant information about children may be lost or assumed unimportant.

While early education programs may preach and even practice (within curriculum design and instruction) developmentally appropriate programs that, by definition, includes individualization and modification based upon developmental needs, these programs often use rigid assessment practices that assume homogeneity of rates and styles of learning. This further ex-acerbates a problem that exists in early education today, that of viewing assessment and evaluation as separate from curriculum. As this book has suggested throughout, if early education professionals are to fully integrate curriculum and assessment, then they must fully practice what they preach.

BECOMING INFORMED USERS OF ASSESSMENT TECHNIQUES AND INFORMATION

There are a number of things that early childhood professionals should consider when using tests and interpreting assessment information. Some of these suggestions have their foundation in what has been discussed previously in this book and are meant to serve as a review, while others are meant to serve as a preview of forthcoming discussions in subsequent chapters. In addition, recategorizing the information in this way casts a new light on its significance. These suggestions pertain to the more formal and structured assessment procedures such as standardized and teacher-made tests.

1. Select only tests that have demonstrated validity. It is important to determine that the assessment instrument tests what it purports

to measure. As such, tests should only be used for their intended purposes and in conjunction with other types of assessment information. This is crucial for curriculum planning as well as for determining child progress.

2. Select only tests that have demonstrated reliability. This is important because it ensures that the information garnered from the assessment results are not spurious. Again, for making decisions about children and/or curriculum, be sure that the findings are consistent.

3. Consider readiness test results as only one source of information to assist with appropriate curriculum planning. While the readiness test may indicate where the child's academic performance level is at a given moment, NAEYC (2003) states that children should not have to conform to rigid homogeneous group expectations. Rather, groupings for specific activities should be flexible and change frequently. Therefore, observation of children's performance within group activities serve as important sources of readiness information.

4. Never use test scores as the sole basis to determine placement. Children should be allowed to enter school based upon their legal right to enter and upon their chronological age, not based upon what knowledge they have acquired (Maxwell & Clifford, 2004). Further, NAEYC (2003) contends that promotion and placement in special programs should be based upon multiple sources of information.

5. Gather assessment information about children on a regular basis. Children learn at different rates and do not conform to the rigid schedules for learning sometimes imposed upon them by curriculum and teachers. Therefore, it is important to regularly determine, not simply at the end of an experience, information about children's academic and developmental accomplishments.

It is incumbent upon the educator to become an informed user of tests. In early childhood, the educator must be aware not only of the test's traits but also of the traits of the children for whom the test is intended. In addition, the educator must also understand fully how the test results will be used.

PART III

The Role of Informal Assessment and Evaluation in Early Childhood Education

CHAPTER 7

Informal Assessment and Evaluation Procedures

INFORMAL ASSESSMENT and evaluation procedures include direct observation; the use of interviews, questionnaires, rating scales and checklists; rubrics; and collecting samples of children's actual classroom work. As with other, more formal forms of assessment, there are distinct advantages and disadvantages associated with informal assessment and evaluation measures. Some of the advantages and disadvantages are inherent in the assessment procedure, while others are due to how the assessment information is used or not used.

ADVANTAGES IN USING INFORMAL ASSESSMENT

One distinct advantage in using informal assessment procedures is that the assessments are derived directly from the curriculum and the teacher's instructional objectives or from commercial published curricula (Wortham, 2001). Rather than relying on what a test publisher believes is important to assess in terms of children's learning, teachers are able to choose and assess processes, skills, and knowledge that they deem appropriate and important within the context of the curriculum and instructional goals and objectives.

Another advantage to using informal assessments is that they maintain the integrity of a constructivist approach to teaching and learning. Most formal assessments focus on the determination of whether or not children have acquired particular skills or knowledge, and assess this in isolation from how children use these skills or knowledge in a meaningful context. In contrast, informal assessments are appropriate for assessing the process of how children learn and how they use the knowledge and skills that they have acquired within the context of the activities embedded in the curriculum.

If designed and used appropriately, informal assessments can be correlated with diagnostic needs (Wortham, 2001)—another advantage. If teachers are looking for a means to individualize the curriculum to meet individual children's needs or to group children for more effective instruction, informal assessments can be used for these purposes as well. They give more meaning to children's performance and can suggest concrete ways to modify curriculum for effective instruction.

Finally, informal assessment reflects a flexible approach to assessing children. Informal assessment approaches can be used to determine mastery as well as to determine at what level the child is performing on his or her way to mastery. In this manner, informal assessments will yield information that the teacher can use to design and implement curriculum activities on the way to mastery.

DISADVANTAGES IN USING INFORMAL ASSESSMENT

Just as there are advantages inherent in using informal assessments, there are also inherent disadvantages. These have to do with both the construction of the measures and the misuse of the information that results from using them.

One disadvantage is related to the improper development and implementation of the assessment measure. According to Wortham (2001), the primary concern here is related to the lack of reliability and validity of the assessments. Wortham suggests that if informal assessments are developed and used by teachers or by school districts, that interrater reliability be established. This can be accomplished by a number of teachers using the assessment in order to determine whether or not they get the same results.

Another disadvantage in using informal assessments is related to the misuse of the information that is gathered using the assessment. This type of disadvantage is no different than the disadvantage associated with more formal assessment means. The primary reason for assessing children is to determine their curricular needs and to measure progress. If the assessment information is used for comparing children or for determining eligibility, then even informal assessments can become "high stakes." There is a double jeopardy associated with this danger if the informal assessment is not reliable or valid.

Finally, Wortham (2001) suggests that the major disadvantage in using informal assessments is that teachers are not adequately prepared to develop them or to use the information effectively for curriculum development and modification. Teachers should be aware of their own levels of competence or limitations in developing, implementing, and using informal assessments. They should collaborate with others who are more expert than they if they are unsure about designing or using informal assessments. The following sections focus on different types of informal assessment procedures that can be used singly or combined to assess children in the context of the classroom.

A number of informal assessment procedures can be used singly or combined to assess children in the context of the classroom. These include direct observation, checklists, rating scales, children's work samples, and rubrics. Each of these methods will be discussed below.

DIRECT OBSERVATION

Direct observation, the most basic of all informal assessment techniques, requires active participation on the teacher's part during daily classroom routines when children are engaged in curricular activities. While teachers often don't trust their powers of observation to inform them about children's strengths and needs, research has demonstrated that when teachers use observation techniques as a basis for their ratings of children's academic strengths, those ratings correlate highly with objective measures of children's academic performance (Gullo & Ambrose, 1987).

According to Wortham (2001), observation procedures afford teachers the opportunity to assess certain behaviors in young children that more formal assessment procedures do not. In early childhood education, teachers are often more concerned with children's learning processes or the processes they use to acquire new information, rather than with what specific information has been learned. More formal test formats do not allow one to determine the processes that occur in young children's minds. Therefore, observations of children solving problems or sorting objects should give greater insights into these processes than do test scores alone.

Moreover, young children have often not mastered the language or behaviors required to perform adequately in a structured test situation. Therefore, observing them in a more natural environment may give a better indication of their competence.

Finally, observation procedures offer a better channel to evaluate children's development than do formal assessments, and early childhood educators are particularly interested in assuring that there is a match between the child's development and educational goals and materials. Therefore, a reliable and valid procedure for assessing development becomes a vital aspect of assessment and evaluation in early education.

Forms of Observation

Observation can take many forms. The form selected should be suited to the situation and setting, as well as to the teacher's skills and needs. Each of the different types of observation appropriate for use in early education will be briefly described.

Anecdotal records. Anecdotal records are brief, narrative descriptions of specific events. According to Boehm and Weinberg (1997), anecdotal records should be used for understanding behavior when there are no other means to evaluate it directly. These behaviors might include such things as attitude toward learning, emotional development, peer relationships, or effects of health on children's adaptation to school settings.

For example, a group of public school, prekindergarten and kindergarten teachers with whom I worked used anecdotal records as a standard procedure in their student assessments. A 5" × 8" note card is kept for each child in the class. The cards for the entire class are held together using a ring-type fastener. Each time the teachers observe something that they have predetermined as important in describing individual progress or in achieving a curricular objective, it is noted on the card. Teachers might note such things as symmetry in block building, patterns established with beads or blocks, colors and designs used in art projects, social interactions between children, or language used.

The teachers use a team approach, and the anecdotal record cards are discussed with aides and specialists who service the rooms. Suggestions for curricular activities, modifications, and further things to look for are typical topics of discussion. The cards are divided into six categories of behaviors, including language and literacy, logic and mathematics, movement, initiative, social relations, and creative representation.

Cartwright and Cartwright (1984) and Goodwin and Driscoll (1980) have suggested a number of characteristics anecdotal records could have as well as procedures for developing them:

1. An anecdotal record should be the result of direct observation of behavior, and the recording should occur as promptly as possible following the event.
2. An anecdotal record should only include the description of a single event.

3. An anecdotal record should include contextual and supportive information to assist in interpretation at a later time.
4. The interpretation of the behaviors observed should be done separately from the recording of behaviors and events described in the anecdotal record.

Running record. A running record is closely related to an anecdotal record, but it is more detailed and represents a sequence of behaviors rather than the description of a single incident. Boehm and Weinberg (1997) note that running records may be useful in describing small changes in development or in behavior. Because the observation is continuous over a specified time period, this procedure can become time consuming. Cryan (1986) suggests that often the use of audio or video recordings of behaviors aid in the process.

Time sampling. Time sampling is used when there is interest in determining the frequency of a certain behavior. In a time sampling procedure, children are observed for a predetermined period during which the specified behavior is recorded each time it occurs. This observational technique may be especially useful for observing children who exhibit problematic behaviors. For example, it might be important to determine how many times a child exhibits aggression or withdrawal during a specific time period, to better plan for their educational needs.

Event sampling. Event sampling is used instead of time sampling when the context is the main point of interest. Rather than observing for behaviors during a specified time period, behaviors are observed during a specified event. Continuing with the example described above, it may be important to know that there are certain contexts when a child exhibits more aggressive outbursts than others. This would provide the teacher with useful environmental information to help plan for that child. Wortham (2001) suggests that one use event sampling when interested in determining cause-effect relationships between context and behavior.

For example, the teachers I described above, who use anecdotal record cards, have determined that, for some children, particular settings or contexts might be useful in providing important information. If a child is having difficulty in exhibiting prosocial behaviors during recess, the teachers will make it a point to observe that child every day during recess in order to note the social interaction that occurs.

Analyzing the Observation Situation

According to Vasta (1979), before engaging in any observational technique, one must consider four questions. First, what will be observed? While this seems like a simple question, it can become rather complex. For example, when observing a single child, it is often difficult to determine how much of the other children's behaviors must be observed and recorded to best understand the target child's behavior. It is also important to determine ahead of time what specific behaviors will indicate what the teacher is trying to observe. What is important here is to understand that observation is not synonymous with lack of structure. There need to be clear targets and goals for the observation to be useful.

Second, when will the observations be made? The importance of this question is obvious for event sampling, but there are also important implications for other types of observation. Central to this question are concerns about the length and timing of observation. The child must be observed for some period of time, and it will be important to determine how long a period of time is adequate to provide a representative sample of behavior. Also related is, with what frequency do observations have to be made in order to give an unbiased behavioral sample? If observations are made only in the morning or only in the afternoon, the timing and single opportunity may confound the conclusions based on these observations. Again, these issues must be addressed prior to observation but perhaps can only be resolved during the process itself.

Third, which observational method will be used? In response to this question, the teacher-observers must first determine what kind of information they are seeking and then choose the method of observation that will best give them this information. In many instances a combination of observational methods may best suit the situation.

Finally, how will the accuracy of the observations be verified? While this may be a difficult question to answer, in some ways it is the most important. The observer must determine if what is being recorded as observed is an interpretation of behavior or an actual accounting of behavior. Often the teacher can verify what was observed by involving multiple observers or through multiple source means. That is, the observation of the behavior may simply lead to further questions or conclusions that are best assessed through formal assessment means.

Advantages and Disadvantages of Direct Observation

The use of direct observation of children's classroom behaviors for purposes of assessment has both advantages and disadvantages. One prominent advantage is that as an assessment procedure, observation does not interrupt the process of educating children. Instead, it is accomplished during classroom time while children are engaged in curricular activities. Another advantage is that it represents a means of assessing children while they are engaged in learning activities in a more natural setting. Learning is assessed during the learning process. A third advantage of observation is that it affords an opportunity to assess a child in a variety of contexts. Small-group, large-group, or individual work time present different challenges to children. Observing a child in each context may provide useful information as well as a greater breadth of information for making curricular decisions for that child. Observing a child in a problem-solving situation using concrete materials as well as in a situation using representational materials provides insights into that child's level of logical thinking.

While observation provides vast flexibility, it has some potential disadvantages as well. Questions regarding the validity of observations are sure to arise. That is, how can one be certain that the behavior that is observed really represents what it is interpreted to represent? Therefore, validity is tied to issues surrounding interpretation of the observation. Teachers vary in their observational skill and training. These factors alone may affect the validity of the observation.

Another potential disadvantage is observer bias. If a teacher sets out to observe a certain type of behavior in a child because of preconceived notions about that child, instances of that behavior may be observed and recorded where it really doesn't exist.

Finally, even an accurate observation may be taken out of context. For example, if the context is not readily known or apparent, the motivation for the behavior may be misinterpreted by the teacher-observer.

To illustrate this very important point, I am reminded of the story of the 4-year-old preschooler who was observed during free choice time. The teacher noted that the child chose to paint at the easel almost every day. There was nothing too unusual about this, as many preschool children are drawn to this art medium because of its novelty. What was unusual, the teacher noted in her observation of the child, was that the child used only the color black. The teacher decided to continue this event sampling procedure. For a week, the child painted using only the black paint. The teacher was convinced that this was a sure sign of an emotional problem or a terrible home situation. Now, if the teacher had left it at that, she might have continued to assume that the child was troubled. However, the teacher decided that she should talk to the child's parents and perhaps get to the root of the "problem." The parents were at a loss to explain the cause and suggested that the teacher ask the child directly why he only used black paint. Taking the parents' suggestion, the teacher asked the child (in a gentle manner of course) why he only used black paint when he painted pictures at the easel. "Because it's the only color I can reach," the boy replied, "you put the other colors too high up."

CHECKLISTS

Checklists are instruments used to record and examine sequenced series of behaviors or skills usually directly related to educational or developmental goals. Checklists can be used by teachers to determine what skills children have or what developmental characteristics they currently possess in order to better plan for the next step. According to Wortham (1990), checklists are best used when a great number of behaviors are to be observed.

Checklists can include a variety of descriptive characteristics (Cryan, 1986). These include such behavioral categories as descriptive statements of traits, specific developmental characteristics, social/emotional behaviors, interests, specific academic skills, specific knowledge, or specific concepts. As such, checklists can either describe behaviors of a general nature (e.g., problem-solving skills, social skills, critical thinking skills, attitudinal characteristics) or of a specific nature (e.g., word attack skills, steps in performing a science experiment, skills required to perform a specific motor sequence, concepts required to perform mathematical operations).

Checklists prove particularly useful in preparing children's progress reports. If designed carefully, the progress reports could be a subset or an abbreviated version of the checklists.

Checklists also are helpful in providing information to parents regarding their child's progress. Parents can readily see the developmental sequence of skills, from "not present" to "emerging" to "developing" to "mastery," and where their child is in this sequence as well as how far their child has progressed over time.

Checklists, if well designed and used appropriately, can be a guide to understanding children's development and for developing curriculum. There are advantages to using checklists for these purposes. One advantage is that they are easy to use and provide a method for assessing individual children. It is usually easy to determine if a behavior or skill exists in an individual child, and by using a checklist format, one need only use a check or an x to keep track. A separate checklist could be kept for each child, thereby enhancing the process of individualizing the assessment. Another advantage of using a checklist is that it provides a clear visual image of children's progress. By coding or dating the observations, it is easy to determine how children are progressing in the specific areas described on the checklists.

There are also disadvantages to using checklists. If the sequence of skills or concepts do not match the curriculum goals, then the information collected would be useless at best and somewhat damaging to the curriculum at worse. If one makes the assumption that those characteristics described on the checklist must be vital (or they wouldn't be on a checklist), then the curriculum might be inappropriately modified to reflect those characteristics. This difficulty occurs primarily when commercially available predetermined developmental or academic checklists are used. The other side of the coin is that teachers must have a thorough understanding of the sequence of behaviors or skills required to perform a task or produce a product when they construct their own checklists. This takes careful research on the part of the teacher or a committee responsible for the instrument construction.

Finally, Wortham (2001) cautions that checklists are not, in and of themselves, assessment instruments. Rather they are an organizing mechanism for describing curriculum or developmental sequences. What is important is how the teacher uses the information regarding what characteristics or traits are present or absent in a child to develop curriculum activities for that child.

RATING SCALES

Rather than documenting the existence or nonexistence of particular behaviors or traits in children, rating scales are used to describe the degree to which those behaviors or traits are believed to be present in the individual. Rating scales are often used to measure those traits not easily described using other assessment procedures. For example, on report cards children's conduct, motivation, effort, and ability to get along with others is often described using a type of rating scale. The child may be rated in each of those areas using the following:

1–Superior
2–Above average
3–Average
4–Below average
5–Unsatisfactory

The major difficulty, and therefore an inherent problem, is that the ratings can become very subjective. Also, there may be descriptive terms used in the rating scales that have ambiguous references, and this increases the incidence of subjectivity.

Both checklists and rating scales describe behaviors without addressing how they are influenced by possible causes or contexts. Therefore, checklists and rating scales are best used in conjunction with other observational forms to provide a more comprehensive assessment picture.

SAMPLES OF CHILDREN'S WORK

Collecting samples of children's actual classroom work is another example of informal assessment. One way of systematizing examples of children's work for purposes of assessment is organizing it into a portfolio. Creating portfolios as an organizational method is discussed in detail in Chapter 8.

There are a number of advantages associated with using collections of children's work. According to Cryan (1986), children's work provides teachers with real and direct rather than contrived evidence of their progress or evidence that is extrapolated from a means other than classroom material. Further, if the examples of work are collected and dated, they may be later used and interpreted by individuals other than the teacher who collected the work.

Decker and Decker (1980), however, suggest that there are potential disadvantages to using actual examples of children's work. One potential disadvantage is storage. Given the number of children in a classroom multiplied by the number of representative examples of classroom work, the amount of material to be collected and stored, even for a short while, could become staggering. One way to solve this problem is to use technology such as computer scanners. Then pictures, writing samples, and examples of problems could be scanned and kept on a disk until a printed copy is needed.

Another disadvantage is that it is difficult to know how many samples or which samples are representative of the child's competence. While informal assessment and evaluation procedures have demonstrated potential for use in early childhood education, mere collections of information may prove cumbersome and confusing. A difficulty in using informal assessment techniques lies in designing an organizational structure for increasing utility and meaningfulness. Alternative assessment techniques, as described in Chapter 8, have been one way early childhood education professionals are trying to surmount some of these difficulties.

RUBRICS

Rubrics are a quantitative measure applied to children's actual work for the purpose of assessment. According to Wiggins (1996),

> A rubric is a printed set of guidelines that distinguishes performances or products of different quality. . . . A rubric has descriptors that define what to look for at each level of performance. . . . Rubrics also often have indicators providing specific examples or tell-tale signs of things to look for in work. (p. VI-5-1)

Wortham (2001) describes three types of rubrics that can be used by teachers in the classroom. The first type of rubric is a *holistic rubric*. A holistic rubric yields a single score that is applied to the child's overall performance. Competency labels define levels of performance. Examples of such labels might be: emergent, developing, beginning, experienced, exceptional. These labels could be applied to overall performance in specific areas such as number recognition, writing, reading, and the like.

Another type of rubric is an *analytic rubric*. "An analytic rubric describes and scores each of the task attributes separately, uses limited descriptors for each attribute, uses a scale that can be both narrow and broad, and allows for specific diagnostic feedback" (Wiener & Cohen, 1997, p. 249). This type of rubric is more specific than a holistic rubric and can be used as an assessment for diagnostic purposes. For example, if the teacher is trying to assess a child's ability to solve a mathematical problem using addition, an analytic rubric could be applied in the following manner:

1—No attempt to solve the problem
2—Completely misinterprets the problem
3—Understands a small part of the problem
4—Understands most of the problem
5—Completely understands the problem and solves it correctly

The third type of rubric is called a *developmental rubric*. A developmental rubric is one that can be used across age levels and focuses on the idea that mastery is a developmental process that may not occur at the same age level or grade level for all children. The developmental rubric may span more than one grade level. Say, for example, the teacher is trying to assess children's ability to use logical thinking in their problem solving. The assumption is that children are at different levels in this ability and might be assessed using the following developmental rubric:

- Classifies and orders objects
- Compares and contrasts objects
- Organizes information
- Forms concepts
- Draws conclusions
- Analyzes concepts
- Synthesizes ideas
- Estimates

According to Wortham (2001), there are both advantages and disadvantages in using rubrics. There are several advantages: (a) Rubrics are flexible and can be used for many uses, grade levels, and ability levels.

(b) They are adaptable and are subject to revision and refinement. (c) Both teachers and children can use rubrics as a means of guiding performance. (d) They can be translated into grades if necessary.

There may be disadvantages in using rubrics as well. One of the major difficulties associated with using rubrics is that teachers may not be skillful in developing the criteria for scoring (Wortham, 2001). Thus teachers may put too much focus on inappropriate criteria, or they may put too much focus on the quantity of criteria rather than on the actual indicators of quality of the children's work. Also certain types of rubrics may lack reliability and validity: The quality indicators may be too general and thus too difficult to use effectively as a rating of the quality of the child's work.

In this chapter, a number of informal assessment and evaluation strategies were described and discussed. Advantages and disadvantages in using these strategies were delineated. In Chapter 8, a specific type of informal assessment will be the focus, namely, performance-based assessment.

Assessment Using Performance-Based Strategies

ONE WAY EARLY childhood professionals address the issue of testing and assessment as well as the manner in which it fits into a curriculum that meets children's developmental needs is through assessment procedures that rely on performance-based activities embedded within the context of classroom activities. This type of assessment is also referred to as alternative or authentic assessment.

Alternative or *authentic* assessment are terms to describe the types of assessment procedures and organizational structures that are being used in lieu of or in addition to standardized testing, or paper and pencil tests. These types of assessments are more descriptive in nature and take various forms. Rather than simply focusing on the products of learning (e.g., the right answers), they emphasize and strive to portray how children process information, construct new knowledge, and solve problems.

It should be noted that alternative or authentic assessment describes an organizational approach, not a specific procedure. It does not reinvent the wheel. Rather, it is an approach to assessment that helps individuals organize and make sense out of some of the various types of informal assessment procedures discussed in Chapter 7. An alternative assessment approach provides the vehicle through which these various types of assessment procedures can be integrated and used in concert to describe children's progress. Several alternative or performance-based assessment approaches are used in early childhood programs.

CURRICULUM-BASED ASSESSMENT

Curriculum-based assessment describes a wide-ranging approach for alternative assessment that directly links the assessment process to the curriculum content and instructional strategies used within the early childhood classroom (Cohen & Spenciner, 1994). According to Bergen (1997), assessing a child within the learning context is extremely useful and informative. Specifically, assessing a child within the learning context makes it possible to assess the child-context variables that may affect the learning capacity and the demonstration of learning for that child (Bergen & Mosley-Howard, 1994). This proves useful for curriculum planning and modification. With young children, it may be observed that learning within a specific context may be different from day to day, and all of these factors must be taken into account when assessing the child's learning.

According to Cohen and Spenciner (1994), curriculum-based assessment has three distinct purposes:

1. To determine eligibility of a child for participating in specific curriculum and learning experiences
2. To develop the specific curriculum and instruction goals for that child based on his or her performance within the classroom context
3. To assess the child's progress as he or she proceeds through the curriculum

Within a curriculum-based assessment procedure, the child's behavior in developmental, social, preacademic, or academic areas are used as the basis for assessing the child. The information gleaned from this process is then used to make modifications to the curriculum that are more suited to the child and his or her level of development or academic capacity.

Curriculum-based assessment is a process that involves a number of distinct yet interrelated steps. The primary assumption of this process is that the teacher knows the curriculum, what is being taught, and how what is being taught is presented to the children. The process involves the following steps:

- The teacher develops and uses a system for curriculum-based assessment that provides a direct connection to the curriculum and instruction practices used within the classroom context.
- The teacher uses the results of the curriculum-based assessment to modify the curriculum and instructional practices, ensuring that a child's developmental and academic needs are being met.
- After modifications are instituted, the child is assessed again within the modified curricular context.

- The teacher determines whether the modifications have benefited the child in the intended manner.
- The process repeats itself in a dynamic fashion.

A special application of curriculum-based assessment is curriculum-based language assessment (Mindes, 2003). This particular application is used when the teacher is not sure that a child has the linguistic capacity to function adequately within the curriculum that is being used in the classroom. This is particularly useful in helping the teacher bridge the gap between the linguistic capacity of the child and the kinds of demands that are being placed on the child by the curriculum.

Research has demonstrated that the use of curriculum-based assessment is effective in a number of ways in early childhood classrooms. One of the primary findings is that curriculum-based assessment, when applied appropriately, leads to educators being able to amend and align their instruction to meet the individual needs of students in their classrooms (Phillips, Fuchs, & Fuchs, 1994). The result of this is that curriculum-based assessment improves teaching practice.

One study found that curriculum-based assessment could be used to establish academic growth benchmarks for young children with learning disabilities in the area of literacy: Young children who had curriculum-based assessment, as compared to children who did not, had growth rates on grade-level reading performance of 1.39 words gained per week as compared to 0.5 words gained per week (Deno, Fuchs, Marston, & Shin, 2001). The investigators concluded from their analysis of effective intervention research that children with learning disabilities could achieve rates of growth that were comparable to those of their classroom peers who were not identified as learning disabled and that the enhanced rates were attributable to the curriculum-based assessment approach. Curriculum-based assessment revealed specific interventions that were sufficiently efficient to individual children.

In another study, VanDerHeyden, Witt, Naquin and Noell (2001) reported that curriculum-based assessment was effective in identifying kindergarten children with deficiencies in readiness skills. They found that curriculum-based assessment was both a reliable and a valid assessment procedure to scrutinize readiness in kindergarten children, and they suggest using curriculum-based assessment as a screening device within the context of the classroom.

PLAY-BASED ASSESSMENT

It is often said that play is at the heart of the early childhood curriculum, especially for children at the younger age ranges. For young children, play is voluntary and intrinsically motivating. When teachers systematically observe children at play, they can gain valuable insights into developmental and academic competencies.

According to Mindes (2003), it is the teacher in the assessor's role that makes this approach to assessment work. As the assessor, the early childhood educator makes numerous decisions during the assessment process:

- When to change the play props
- What kinds of props to use
- When to add stimulation to the play theme
- When to mediate
- When to actively engage in the play process
- When to end the play process

According to Van Hoorn, Nourot, Scales, and Alward (1999), one of the easiest ways for early childhood educators to begin assessing children utilizing a play-based approach is to make a list of critical skills and applications of knowledge and then match this list to the curriculum goals and objectives. They offer the following as examples of how a teacher could use curriculum-assessment matches:

- Prepare a play-based assessment observation log that is keyed to various learning areas and social contexts within the classroom.
- Keep track of where a child plays in the classroom.
- Document whether a child plays alone, with one other child, or with two or more children.
- List stages of play with various objects and in various activities for each child in the class; then note how each child is progressing through these stages.
- Keep track of the role of play for each child. For example, how does a child use props? Engage in make-believe activities? Engage in social interaction during play? Use language/communication play?

Using play activities as a means of assessing the child's knowledge and skills is not entirely a new phenomenon. Teachers have long been observing children during play and making decisions about them based on those observations. Much of the research on play-based assessment, however, has been done on young children with special needs.

Bricker, Pretti-Frontczak, and McComas (1998) suggest making a chart with specific categories to use with young children who have special needs. They suggest using the following categories:

- Fine and gross motor abilities
- Cognitive skills
- Social interaction
- Interactive communication
- Self-help and self-care skills

They also suggest that this approach be integrated into the planned curriculum activities that are designed to meet the individual goals for the child. The information from this particular type of approach can then be used for further intervention, curriculum modification, and individualized planning.

Calhoon (1997) studied young children with language delays in order to determine the effectiveness of a play-based assessment approach in analyzing children's language capabilities. The author concluded that a play-based assessment approach provided a much broader picture of children's linguistic capabilities as compared to other assessment approaches. In addition, it was found that the play-based approach also yielded more helpful information in planning curricular modifications and interventions.

In a similar study, Farmer-Dougan and Kaszuba (1999) compared a play-based assessment model to standardized assessment of cognition and social skills in preschool children. The authors found that the findings gleaned from the play-based assessment accurately reflected the children's level of cognitive and social functioning.

It has also been shown that the play context may affect the assessment outcome. Malone (1994) conducted a study with preschool children having cognitive delays. The children in the study were observed at home during independent play and at school during group free play. It was found that the children's assessed developmental age was more predictive of the behaviors during the independent play episodes at home than in the group free play episodes at school. The author suggests that these findings highlight the need to consider that variations in behavior may be associated with the specific play context.

Finally, Myers, McBride, and Peterson (1996) conducted a study to ascertain the relative efficacy of play-based assessment as compared to other forms of assessment. In this study, preschool children who were referred for special education were randomly assigned to either a multidisciplinary, standardized assessment or a play-based assessment group. The results of the study found that play-based assessments took less time to complete and had a high congruence with other forms of developmental ratings. In addition, the play-based assessment group also resulted in more favorable parent and staff perceptions and provided more useful reports.

DYNAMIC ASSESSMENT

Dynamic assessment is a form of alternative assessment that can be combined with other forms of assessments. In this type of assessment, the learner is directly engaged in the learning process by using mediated learning experiences. Mediated learning experiences are the foci of dynamic assessment (Cohen & Spenciner, 1994).

This approach utilizes a test-intervene-retest design. A mediated learning experience can be described as an interaction that takes place between an assessor and a child. The assessor mediates the environment to the child through appropriate framing, selecting, focusing, and feeding back to the child the experiences that the child is having. The purpose in doing this is to produce in the child appropriate learning systems and routines. Actual curriculum activities comprise the assessment tasks that are presented to the child. Thus the approach combines both assessment and teaching. Dynamic assessment is a procedure that was designed by Reuven Feuerstein (1979, 1980) and is based upon the theoretical work of Vygotsky (1978, 1986).

One of the most useful aspects of Vygotsky's theory in this assessment approach is the Zone of Proximal Development (ZPD). According to Vygotsky (1978), there is a difference between those things that the child can accomplish alone and those things that the child can accomplish with the assistance of someone at a higher developmental level. The ZPD represents the zone in which the child requires assistance to accomplish a task. According to Bodrova and Leong (1996), a teacher can utilize the ZPD through the observation of children to determine their progress toward skill mastery. What is important here for an effective use of the ZPD is that the teacher has an understanding of how a child learns and develops so that he or she is able to determine what kinds of experiences or assistance the child will require to get to the next step in the developmental sequence (Wortham, 2001). As such, curriculum practice is affected by this approach.

Lidz (1991) describes three components comprising the dynamic assessment approach:

1. The assessor actively facilitates learning in a child while engaging the child in active participation in the learning task.
2. Evaluation of the process is the primary emphasis of the assessment procedure. A major focus is on metacognitive processes that the child uses in learning. The teacher-assessor uses questions, suggestions, and prompts to help the child better understand, on a conscious level, what and how he or she is learning.

3. The results of the assessment yields information on how change can be produced in the child and how malleable the child is within the learning context.

According to Mindes (2003), the dynamic assessment approach is particularly useful for early childhood teachers who are interested in linking classroom instruction to specific learner outcomes. Mindes states that "the approach links test results to task analysis to teaching to individualization of instruction. It is an opportunity for making the learning process apparent to those children who may need special assistance in linking thinking to academic requirements" (p. 159).

A number of studies have been conducted examining the efficacy of dynamic assessment as compared to other forms of assessment or how it added to the information yielded from different assessment systems. In one study Jacobs (2001) found that by incorporating dynamic assessment components in a computerized preschool language-screening test, the computerized assessment was enhanced and continued investigation of its validity was possible.

In another study (Bolig & Day, 1993), it was found that dynamic assessment could be used to respond to the criticism of traditional intelligence tests, inasmuch as it could be used to identify children's learning ability, determine how and what to teach to children, and assess giftedness in culturally diverse children and children from homes of economic poverty. In addition, they found that through the use of dynamic assessment, individual differences could be controlled and different domains of giftenedness could be identified and explored.

In one study, examining the effects of dynamic assessment on content-specific material, Jitendra and Kameenui (1993) found that children at different levels of mathematical performance could be identified. In their study of third graders, they found that dynamic assessment indicated important and significant differences between novices and experts in their ability to use specific mathematical strategies for solving problems.

In another study, Spector (1992) found that dynamic assessment was able to measure phonemic awareness to predict progress in beginning reading. This study, conducted with kindergartners, supported the utility of the developed measures and was able to demonstrate the applicability of the principles of dynamic assessment to the measurement in kindergarten-aged children.

There have also been studies utilizing dynamic assessment procedures that were conducted with young children with special needs. Findings from these studies have implications for both teachers and children. Delclos (1987) found that after teachers viewed dynamic assessment situations, their academic expectations for cognitively delayed children were raised. Lidz and Pena (1996) compared dynamic assessment to traditional assessment for determining language delays among Latino preschool children. They found that there was increased accuracy among teachers in their ability to assess children's language abilities using dynamic assessment.

PROJECT ASSESSMENT

Project assessment is another type of alternative assessment that is used to assess children's academic progress through the assessment of their knowledge and problem-solving skills by observing them in actual problem-solving situations. These problem-solving situations are actual activities that are part of the curriculum. One example of a project assessment procedure is Project Spectrum (Krechevsky, 1991, 1998). The strategy put forth in Project Spectrum is to recognize that there is potential variation in all children and in all curriculum activities. The goal of assessment in Project Spectrum is to identify a child's domain—specific strengths in an area not necessarily addressed in more traditional assessment systems.

Project Spectrum is based on the theoretical foundation of Gardner's (1983) multiple intelligences theory. Gardner (1999) suggests that teachers should provide children with various avenues to become engaged in curriculum content and with multiple opportunities for developing and demonstrating understanding and competence. In addition, teachers should utilize varied products and processes for assessing children and documenting their work.

According to Krechevsky (1991), "It is the responsibility of the educational system to discover and nurture proclivities. Rather than building around a test, the Spectrum approach is centered on a wide range of rich activities; assessment comes about as part-and-parcel of the child's involvement over time in these activities" (p. 44).

There are a number of Project Spectrum characteristics that are consistent with the features of developmentally appropriate practice:

- The curriculum and assessment procedures become integrated. Early childhood practices that are developmentally appropriate view the relationship between curriculum and evaluation as transactional, that is, each simultaneously affects the other. By using activities embedded within the curriculum as a means to evaluate, and by using the outcome of the evaluation as a method to modify the curriculum, this relationship becomes actualized.
- The procedure embeds assessment into real-word activities that are meaningful to children. By putting the problem-solving activity into

a context for which children have referents in reality, one is more likely to maintain the interest and motivation necessary to obtain valid and reliable results.

- The procedures used are intelligence-fair—they do not rely solely or primarily on language and logical thinking. Also, children's styles of performance are identified. Just as children do not develop in compartmentalized ways, they also do not learn or demonstrate competence in this manner. And just as the curriculum must be sensitive to the multiple modes of learning that children use to acquire and construct knowledge, evaluation must be similarly sensitive.
- The procedures used identify and emphasize children's strengths. Rather than focus on what children don't know and can't do, they focus on what they can do and do know, and this allows one to approach evaluation and subsequent curriculum development from a positive vantage point. The modus operandi is that all children can learn.

The utilization of this assessment approach has been studied to determine its efficacy as compared to other forms of assessment. Importantly, Chen (1998) found that the core method for assessing child progress on curriculum activities is teacher observation. Hatch and Gardner (1996) have demonstrated that this approach to assessment is useful and valid in assessing the pluralistic abilities of each individual child as compared to more standardized forms of assessment.

Another study (Wexler-Sherman, Gardner, & Feldman, 1988) showed that the project approach to assessment was successful in fusing assessment with curriculum within a preschool setting, by comparing the project assessment approach to other more standard forms of assessment in this pilot project. Hebert (1992) examined the utilitarian characteristics of this approach as compared to more standardized assessment modes. It was found that by using a project assessment approach, the assessment process became more meaningful through using learning experiences.

Finally, Vialle (1994) conducted a study with child care centers for children who came from homes of economic poverty. It was found that this framework for assessment is productive for all children, and is especially appropriate for children who reflect atypical profiles of intelligence.

PORTFOLIO ASSESSMENT

The National Association for the Education of Young Children (Bredekamp & Rosegrant, 1992) defines *assessment* as "the process of observing, recording, and otherwise documenting the work that children do and how they do it, as a basis for a variety of educational decisions that affect the child" (p. 10).

One way in which early childhood professionals have responded to the need for an assessment process that fits within the paradigm of developmentally appropriate practice, and the need to view assessment data as useful information for educational decision making, has been to use the actual work done by students within the context of the curriculum as the basis for assessing children's knowledge and skills. The need for a tool that would enable the teacher to methodically collect and organize those materials that were deemed useful in describing the progress that children were making, both developmentally and academically, grew out of this movement. Portfolios became the solution.

According to Vavrus (1990), portfolios are a systematic and organized collection of the work that children do as they are engaged in classroom activities. The child's work that is represented in the portfolio reflects curriculum goals, content, and strategies. It should be noted that portfolios are not, in and of themselves, an assessment tool. Rather, they provide a convenient way to organize and store the information that is gathered about children.

According to Sewell, Marczak, and Horn (2003), portfolio assessment is widely used in educational settings as a means for examining and measuring children's progress. This is accomplished by documenting the learning process as it occurs naturally within the classroom context. Portfolio assessment is based on the principle that children should demonstrate what they know and what they do (Cole, Ryan, & Kick, 1995). Demonstrating what they know and can do can be contrasted with indicating with paper and pencil what they know, which is more typical in formal assessments such as teacher-made tests or standardized tests.

Research has shown that portfolio assessment is effective and useful in a number of ways. Benson and Smith (1998), in an in-depth qualitative study, found that first-grade teachers who utilized a portfolio approach to assessment realized a number of benefits. The study demonstrated that teachers

- Found portfolios were beneficial as a means of communicating more effectively with children's families about the kinds of progress their child was making in the class. (In an earlier study with kindergarten teachers, Diffily and Fleege [1994] had shown that kindergarten teachers found portfolios helpful in reporting children's progress to parents.)
- Viewed portfolios as an effective tool to motivate, encourage, and instruct children in their classrooms in the skills of self-assessment.

- Saw portfolios as a mechanism to monitor and improve their own instructional skills and curriculum modification.

In another study with teachers, Shaklee and Viechnicki (1995) found that portfolio assessment was an effective model for assessing children as exceptional learners, as well as assessing their ability to use, generate, and pursue knowledge. They also noted that the portfolio model of assessment was efficacious in terms of credibility, transferability, dependability, and confirmability.

Sewell et al. (2003) cite instances in which portfolio assessment is most useful and instances in which portfolio assessment may not be particularly useful. The usefulness of portfolio assessment depends on how one plans to use the information as well as on the characteristics of the programs that the children who are being assessed attend. Portfolio assessment is most useful for the following:

- Evaluating program goals and outcomes that are flexible or individualized for children
- Evaluating programs that value the individuals involved as being part of program change or making decisions related to personal change
- Providing meaningful information related to the process of behavioral change over time
- Providing a means of communicating with a wide range of audiences regarding program accountability or child progress
- Providing a possible means of assessing more complex aspects of behavioral change, rather than simply measuring those behavioral changes that are most easily measured

There are also instances where portfolio assessment may not be the most efficacious means of documentation. These include the following:

- Assessing children's behavior in programs where the goals are very concrete and are uniform for all children who participate in the program
- Assessing children where the purpose is to rank them quantitatively or in a standardized manner
- Assessing children for the purpose of comparing them to one another using standardized norms

Purposes of a Portfolio

Portfolios provide a useful and practical means for early childhood educators to examine children's strengths, in their developmental and learning processes and progress. Portfolios also provide a means for targeting those areas of development and achievement where there is a need for support. Shanklin and Conrad (1991) describe portfolios as a means by which educational professionals become empowered as decision makers. By developing a portfolio system for collecting information about children, teachers are able to determine what information is important to collect, what type of analysis protocol is appropriate, how the information resulting from the analyses will be used for decision making and curriculum modification, and how the information will be shared with others.

The information about children's developmental status and educational achievement found in portfolios has many uses for the early childhood educator (Nall, 1994; Shepard, 1989). There are also many benefits for teachers, children, and families that result from this method of assessment. It is difficult to differentiate the uses from the benefits. Often, the way in which the information contained in the portfolio is used becomes the benefit. A number of these uses and benefits are discussed below.

Focus on change. The information gathered for the portfolio, mainly in the form of documentation of children's learning processes or the actual products that children produce as a result of engaging in curriculum activities, allows the teacher to focus on the changes in development and achievement that occur in children over time. By examining these processes and products, teachers are able to chart children's progress throughout the curriculum and over time. In this manner, the information gathered as part of the portfolio permits teachers to focus both on children's developmental and educational processes as well as on products.

Focus on individualized instruction. As noted above, the records of children's learning processes and curriculum products contained in portfolios, when used properly, permit early childhood educators to compare children's progress. The progress that is charted is not compared to how other children are progressing, but rather, the comparative measure is the same child. As such, portfolio assessment focuses on the individual child rather than on groups of children. Children's progress is measured against their own rate of acquisition and development of knowledge and skills. This information can be used to make appropriate modifications in the curriculum in response to children's strengths and needs. Because the focus is on the individual child, collecting assessment data based on actual performance in curriculum activities as a means of documenting developmental and academic progress doesn't rely on a one-chance opportunity for children to demonstrate competence. Information is collected on a regular basis, and often. In this manner, teachers have several opportunities to observe and record children's behaviors in various contexts. This improves both the reliability and validity of the assessment and better ensures that what is being observed accurately reflects the child's capabilities.

Focus on the curriculum. It is important that any assessment closely reflects the content and the instructional strategies that are part of the everyday classroom teaching. Using activities that reflect what the child actually does in the curriculum as assessment tools provides such a match. The resulting assessment data are, therefore, germane for subsequent curriculum development and adjustment. When used appropriately, the materials contained in the portfolio provide a concrete and systematic means for modification of the curriculum. The purposes of this are twofold: It not only supports the individual needs of the child, but also helps teachers recognize in a more general manner, what works and what doesn't work in the curriculum as it is being implemented—in terms of both content and instruction. Additionally, when curriculum-based activities and products are collected for assessment purposes, this form of assessment does not interrupt the process of curriculum implementation. According to Maness (1992), teachers spend approximately 14 hours per year preparing their students to take standardized tests, 26 hours reading tests, and 18 hours preparing teacher-made assessment measures. If collected and used appropriately, the information collected for portfolios does not require time out from "teaching" the curriculum.

Focus on teacher and child reflection. Both teachers and children participate in the process of collecting information that is to be included in portfolios. In this manner, teachers and children increase their opportunities to reflect on those things that are part of the teaching-learning process. Teachers should encourage children to select their "best" work to include in the portfolio. By doing this, children become aware of their own accomplishments. Through this process, teachers gain valuable insights into how children view their own competencies and accomplishments. Teachers can reflect on the ways in which the curriculum serves the needs of the children by discussing portfolio entries with them. When both teachers and children become full participants in the process of collecting materials for inclusion in portfolios, they increase the number of opportunities for learning about themselves in the process of teaching and learning.

Focus on sharing information with others. When curriculum activities and materials are used as the basis of evidence used to assess children, they provide concrete and meaningful information to present to parents, other teachers, administrators, and other pertinent members of the public sector. These types of materials allow the teacher to focus on what progress children have made by presenting actual examples of their work. In this manner, others will gain a better understanding of the developmental progression of where children started, how far they have progressed, and where they will go next in the curricular process. This process also gives others who are not directly involved a better understanding of the curriculum—what are the goals and outcomes expected as well as why particular teaching strategies, materials, and activities are utilized.

Documentation is one example of how the work of a child is shared with others. Developed in the preschools of Reggio Emilia, Italy, and in the United States, documentation is viewed as communication (Cadwell, 2002; Helm, Beneke, & Steinheimer, 1998). As such, documentation serves multiple purposes:

- Making families aware of their child's experiences
- Allowing teachers to better understand the children in their classrooms
- Allowing teachers to evaluate their own work with children
- Allowing teachers to share information with other teachers
- Showing children that their work is valued

Variation in Portfolio Types

There are three variations of portfolios that are most used in the field of early childhood education (Mills, 1989; Vermont Department of Education, 1988, 1989). The first variation is called the *works-in-progress portfolio*. The works-in-progress portfolio contains stories, artwork, problem-solving examples, and the like, that children are currently working on. Depending on the types of work collected and the frequency with which work is collected, this type of portfolio can become unmanageable within a short amount of time. The works-in-progress portfolio can potentially contain all of the work that the child is doing. Because of its "richness," it can soon lose its potential for assessment.

The second portfolio variation is called the *current-year portfolio*. The current-year portfolio contains particular selections of work that are mutually agreed on for inclusion by the teacher and the child. The work contained in the current-year portfolio must meet certain criteria. These are the curriculum products that are then scrutinized by teachers in order to elucidate for them children's levels of accomplishments. This particular type of portfolio also gives teachers a better understanding of how to structure or restructure the curriculum for the child's next step.

The third variation is called the *permanent portfolio*. Contained in the permanent portfolio are highly selected examples of a child's curriculum products. The permanent portfolio will accompany the child to his or her next class. While the number of examples of a child's work that are contained in the permanent portfolio needs to be limited, they should, at the same time, provide the receiving teacher with a clear understanding of the child's developmental and academic accomplishments from the previous year.

Contents of a Portfolio

Information included in portfolios as documentation of behavioral changes in children should be collected from multiple sources, through multiple methods, and over multiple points in time (Shaklee, Barbour, Ambrose, & Hansford, 1997). While there are many types of items that can be selected to be included in a child's portfolio, the items should reflect the work that the child does spontaneously as a part of the curriculum. At times it is not possible to include the actual product, such as block constructions, and a photograph or a description of the work would be substituted.

Samples of children's work. According to Meisels and Steele (1991), actual samples of children's work should comprise the major contents of a portfolio. These samples may take different forms and include such things as writing examples, artwork, and mathematical calculations. In addition, photographs or other media can be included to record the child's work. Importantly, the work samples should be dated so that progress can be documented. Attempts should be made to include samples from all parts of the school year—the beginning, middle, and end. Teachers should also take great care to insure that the samples are representative of the many types of opportunities that are available to the child in the classroom. Additionally, efforts should be made to include examples that represent efforts that take place in multiple curriculum and classroom contexts. Work representing all areas of the curriculum should be included in the portfolio. It should be cautioned that it is easy to overrepresent those areas that are paper and pencil type tasks. The teacher should choose some of the work that is included in the portfolio, and the child should select some as well.

There are both advantages and disadvantages in using examples of children's actual work. According to Cryan (1986), the actual work of children provides the early childhood professional with real and direct, rather than contrived or extrapolated, evidence of children's progress. In addition, if the samples are collected and dated, as suggested above, they can be interpreted and used at a later date by individuals other than the teacher who collected the work.

According to Decker and Decker (1980), there may also be some prospective disadvantages in using children's actual classroom work as assessment. One potential disadvantage is storage. This particular issue was briefly addressed earlier in the chapter. Given the number of children in a classroom, multiplied by the number of samples of work collected as representative, the amount of material that is to be stored could become unmanageable. A potential resolution to this problem would be to use advanced technology, such as computer scanners. Thus pictures, writing samples, and examples of problems could be scanned and kept on a disk until a printed copy is needed.

A second potential disadvantage to using the actual work of children is that it is difficult to know how many samples, or which samples, are accurately representative of the child and his or her capabilities and potential. While there are potential disadvantages, the advantages of using children's work outweigh them.

Anecdotal records. As mentioned above, there are times when it is not suitable to include the actual work of the child. At these times, it becomes necessary to incorporate a description of the work into the portfolio. This is especially true if the work is deemed significant in documenting developmental or academic progress. One appropriate method would be to use an anecdotal record to detail this information. An anecdotal record is a brief, narrative description of an event. Anecdotal records should be used especially if no other means are available to document and understand an event (Boehm & Weinberg, 1997). Events such as problem-solving processes or social interactions that take place during an activity would be appropriately documented using anecdotal records. As with other examples of children's work, anecdotal records should be dated so that developmental progress or advances in academic accomplishments can be noted.

Curriculum checklists. Checklists can be used to document a sequenced series of behaviors or skills that are often linked directly to the educational or developmental goals that are curriculum based. As such, checklists may appropriately be included in a child's portfolio. A discussion of the types of checklists and how they are used can be found in Chapter 7.

Other portfolio items. There are also other means of representing the actual work that children do. These also are appropriate for inclusion in children's portfolios. These include, but are not limited to audiotapes, videotapes, reading logs, conference records, and test results. These items will add to the richness of the information that can be obtained from the previous examples of children's work described.

Criteria for Including Children's Work in Portfolios

When making decisions about which examples of children's work to include in the child's portfolio, a number of criteria should be considered (Shanklin & Conrad, 1991). Teachers should ask themselves the following three questions when deciding what to place into children's portfolios:

1. What will the samples of children's work tell me about their level of development and academic progress?
2. How will the information obtained from the samples of children's work help me make decisions about curriculum development, individualization, and modification?
3. How does the actual process of collecting the samples of children's work assist the children in understanding their own developmental and academic accomplishments?

Paulson, Paulson, and Meyer (1991) point out that portfolios should have some type of common structure across all children. It is through this structure that they become effective and useful for instruction and curriculum development. A rationale, goals, standards, and a systematized procedure for selecting and collecting work samples should be considered an integral part of that structure.

Finally, the function of the portfolio may change from the beginning of the academic experience to the end of the academic experience. The work collected over that time span, measuring developmental change and academic progress may differ from the work that is passed on to the next teacher as the best evidence of change over time.

WORK SAMPLING SYSTEM

A comprehensive alternative assessment approach is the Work Sampling System (Meisels et al., 2001). This system of assessment contains a number of different features, including developmental guidelines, developmental checklists, specific coverage of all curriculum areas most typically found in places of learning, provisions for summary report development, and a means for portfolio development. The system is a standards-based approach and can be modified to meet all state and local needs, including requirements for children with special educational needs. It is also a good model for exemplifying how children should be included in the process of portfolio development.

The Work Sampling System is made up of three distinct components. Developmental checklists comprise the first component. Through teacher observation, seven developmental/learning domains are documented for each child being assessed:

- Personal and social development
- Language and literacy
- Mathematical thinking
- Scientific thinking
- Social studies
- Art and music
- Physical development

Through the process of completing these checklists, teachers also will gain information about the curriculum since it is the philosophy of this approach that instruction and learning become integrated with the assessment of children. Additionally, through this process, teachers also gain an understanding of the observation process in that guidelines for this understanding are provided.

The development of a portfolio for each child comprises the second component. During this process, both the teacher and the child are actively involved in the selection of the portfolio contents. The items that are chosen to be included in the portfolio represent the seven areas listed above. This process also informs curriculum in that it involves the integration of the teaching and learning process. Items are selected to be included in the portfolio several times a year, and thus it becomes a useful tool for recording, scrutinizing, and summarizing the child's learning and development throughout the school year (Harrington, Meisels, McMahon, Dichtelmiller, & Jablon, 1997; Meisels, 1993).

The third component is a summary report, which is completed for each child three times a year. Using this summary report, teachers report information about the child's progress to parents, and a determination is made whether or not the child is making sufficient progress in all seven domains. Specific criteria are used for determining the progress of the child's performance.

According to Wortham (2001), the Work Sampling System is based on the philosophy that the assessment of children's performance within the context of the curriculum is appropriate in that this approach:

- Documents the child's daily activity
- Reflects an individualized approach to assessment
- Integrates assessment with curriculum and instruction
- Assesses many elements of learning
- Allows teachers to learn how children reconstruct knowledge through interacting with materials and peers (p. 252)

STRATEGIES FOR IMPLEMENTING A
PERFORMANCE-BASED ASSESSMENT PROGRAM

It is important to plan carefully before drastically changing anything perceived as traditional educational practice. Educational evaluation is thought of in narrow terms, and those who have to implement alternative assessment may greet any deviation from traditional practice less than enthusiastically. This is especially true in today's climate of school accountability and the increase in the practice of standardized testing that has become prevalent with the passing of the No Child Left Behind Act. Not until recently has there been any attempt to describe the qualitative differences between assessment and evaluation in early childhood education and assessment and evaluation that occurs in later childhood education years. It is even more recently that an attempt has been made to create evaluation practices that parallel the qualitative differences described. Alternative or authentic assessment is one such attempt.

Although alternative assessment is not limited to a single assessment practice, it is possible to undertake common strategies to insure greater likelihood that the alternative program, however designed, will be successful. One way to measure success is to judge to what extent the program is used.

Create an Assessment Committee

An alternative or performance-based assessment program should be tailored to fit the particular needs of the school, and information should be collected from multiple sources in order to make it fit as closely as possible. Therefore, it is necessary that individuals from diverse backgrounds, who directly and indirectly affect the children and their educational programming, be involved in developing the evaluation plan. Teachers representing each of the grade levels in the school would be essential members of the assessment committee, for they can discern what kinds of information could be collected at any time and what kinds of information would be unique to a particular grade level. They could also anticipate how the evaluation information and procedures fit the existing curriculum. Record keeping is an important part of evaluation, and teachers would be able to foresee how new procedures might be substituted for or added to existing ones.

School administrators are necessary committee members as well. They provide the support, both moral and financial, for school initiatives. Administrators who are convinced of the importance for change in early childhood evaluation will more readily provide such support. In addition, they can provide important feedback for what types of information are necessary for district reporting.

Specialists in music, art, physical education, and other fields can provide important information regarding children's development. As such, they should be included on the committee.

Finally, parent participation is critical. Only parents can provide certain types of information. Unfortunately, parents are accustomed to and expect numerical or letter grades and scores to indicate to them how well their child is doing as compared with others at the same grade or age level. Just as many teachers and administrators need to be convinced that describing children's progress is a viable and valid means of evaluation, parents also need to be educated to this fact. Parents can offer suggestions regarding how this could be done. Their support is fundamental and extremely important.

Develop an Assessment Philosophy

It is imperative that each assessment program or plan have a philosophical basis to it. The philosophy sets the tone and direction. In developing the philosophy, the assessment committee should consider the following questions:

- Why do you assess in early childhood education settings?
- What will you do with the information collected during the evaluation process?
- How are the assessment procedures linked to the curriculum content and implementation strategies?
- What should the information collected during the assessment process tell about the child?
- What should the information collected during the assessment process tell about the curriculum?
- When should assessment take place?
- What is it that will be specifically assessed?
- What decisions about the child will be made as a result of the information gathered?
- What decisions about the curriculum will be made as a result of the information gathered?

By giving detailed responses to these questions, the assessment committee will develop, in essence, evaluation guidelines. These guidelines will, in turn, lead to decisions regarding evaluation materials and procedures.

Develop a Standardized Procedure for Implementation

Developing uniform implementation guidelines for the assessment plan is essential for insuring that it will be used. Because of the largely qualitative nature of the information gathered, there is often the impression that the methods used for collecting and reporting children's personal performance data are unstructured. Therefore, while the specific information gathered on each child may be different, the procedure for gathering it should be standardized. To assist in developing this procedure, a number of things should be considered. The Work Sampling System, described earlier in the chapter, provides a model for such a framework (Meisels et al., 2001).

When should the information be collected? In order to assess developmental change in children, baseline information is essential. This information must be gathered early in the school year, but if gathered too early, those collecting and reporting the information might not be familiar enough with individual children to make valid observations. Therefore, a time early enough in the year to establish baseline, but late enough after the start of school to insure valid observational information, is most beneficial for a first-time observation.

Another issue related to the timing of information collection is curriculum related. If one is interested in evaluating the effectiveness of a particular curriculum experience, it might be important to gather information on all of the children following a specific unit or activity.

How often should the information be collected? In order to assess progress, the spacing of the collection points must be far enough apart to allow development to happen, but not so far apart that something developmentally important that might occur between the collection points is missed. If there are too few collection points, the information will not be as useful for assessing individual children and for modifying the curriculum. If there are too many collection points, the task of assessment becomes too cumbersome and the volume of information collected becomes too great. While the timing of collection points may depend on individual children or individual types of behaviors observed, a common schedule should be drawn for assessing those things designated as critical for reporting progress.

What types of information should be collected? In an alternative assessment plan it is important to specify what types of information will be collected. This information should vary according to the types of knowledge, skills, values, and attitudes that are emphasized in the activities and content areas addressed by the curriculum. Process-oriented as well as product-oriented information should be made part of each child's assessment plan. As stated earlier, both teacher-selected and child-selected material should be included.

Who will collect the information? An alternative assessment program should include multiple sources of information. As such, teachers' descriptions of children's behaviors only represent one of many avenues used to collect information. Thus parents, area specialists, and the children themselves should be considered viable sources. Both formal (e.g., tests, standardized assessments) as well as informal information sources should be included.

What format will be used for reporting the information? Deciding to whom the information will go and for what purpose it will be used are necessary prerequisites for determining the format. A summary progress report in the form of a checklist may be appropriate for parents, but a teacher may need more detailed anecdotal records to determine how the curriculum should be modified to meet the child's developmental needs. Whatever the format, the information should be meaningful, useful, and not overwhelming.

Develop a Plan for Using the Assessment Information

The assessment committee should consider the ways assessment information might be utilized. As explained earlier in the chapter, these could include the following:

1. *Curriculum planning* to develop curriculum activities as well as to modify the curriculum to meet the needs of individual children
2. *Measuring pupil progress* to measure the rate at which individual children are progressing through the curriculum areas as well as the degree to which children are able to effectively use the knowledge they've constructed or acquired
3. *Measuring curriculum effectiveness* to measure the curricular activities' validity in achieving their stated goals and objectives with individuals or groups of children
4. *Reporting information to parents* to provide a reasonable and meaningful amount of concrete evidence to parents regarding their child's progress

As stated above, one of the advantages of using a performance-based assessment is that it doesn't disrupt the process of curriculum implementation. The many developmental and learning activity areas in the early childhood classroom afford teachers many opportunities to engage in assessment and evaluation. In Chapter 9, suggestions are given related to what types of developmental and learning activities might be assessed within various early education classroom contexts.

Integrating Alternative Assessment Procedures into the Early Childhood Curriculum

I T IS OFTEN stated that the curriculum in early childhood education should be integrated (Gullo, 1992). In an integrated curriculum each of the component parts is recognized, in and of itself, for its significance, but each of the components is also recognized as part of a significant whole and, as such, is incorporated into the whole (Kostelnick, Soderman, & Whiren, 2004). The adoption of a curriculum philosophy that includes integration generally means that the curriculum is viewed, either consciously or unconsciously, in a holistic manner.

What exactly are the component parts that become integrated in this approach to curriculum? These can be viewed in different ways. They may be the content areas such as math, social studies, reading/writing/language, and science. They may also be related to implementation of the curriculum, as in the way activities, physical environment, materials, and teacher-child interaction are components of the curriculum. Another way of considering what the component parts of curriculum might look like would be to consider what goes into early childhood program development. In this macroview, the components of early childhood programming might be considered to be curriculum goals and objectives, curriculum development, curriculum implementation, and curriculum and individual evaluation.

This last position will be the focus of this chapter. In the following sections, several areas of developmental and learning activities within the early childhood classroom will be discussed and strategies for integrating performance-based assessment into these areas will be described. Some possible learning outcomes are generated, as well as an elucidation of general and developmental characteristics that might be evident.

In order to illustrate this in a concrete manner, a number of charts will be displayed throughout the chapter. The focus of these illustrations is to demonstrate how each of the possible types of activities often found in early childhood classroom centers might be used to assess different developmental domains and learning outcomes. The activities that will be depicted are art, music and movement, block play, dramatic play, science and discovery, math and manipulatives, and literacy. For each type of activity, suggestions are offered as to which possible developmental domains or learning outcomes might be assessed while observing children engaged in these types of activities. The possible areas of assessment include expressive arts, language arts, mathematical knowledge, scientific knowledge, social studies knowledge, social development, and motor development. Conversely, the charts also are instructive about how development can be enhanced, or what academic skills can be learned or reinforced when a child is engaged in the various activities.

These illustrative charts can be used in two ways. First, as described above, the information from these charts could be used to assess a child's knowledge and skills in particular developmental or academic areas, or to develop checklists, or to help teachers write anecdotal records. The second way in which these charts might be used is to help those who are not teachers in early childhood classrooms better understand what kinds of knowledge and skills children are apt to attain while engaged in activities within these centers. It might be useful to share this information with parents, school administrators, or others who are not in direct contact with young children in the capacity of teaching.

ART ACTIVITIES

Children engaged in art or artlike activities can convey much information concerning their development and their academic skills (see Figure 9.1).

Lowenfeld and Brittain (1975) have identified six developmental stages in children's drawings that are reminiscent of children's levels of cognitive development. Six stages have been identified, along with their approximate age-level expectancies:

1. Random scribbling (1–2½ years old)
2. Controlled scribbling (2½–3½ years old)
3. Naming of scribbling (3½–4 years old)
4. Representation attempts (4–5 years old)

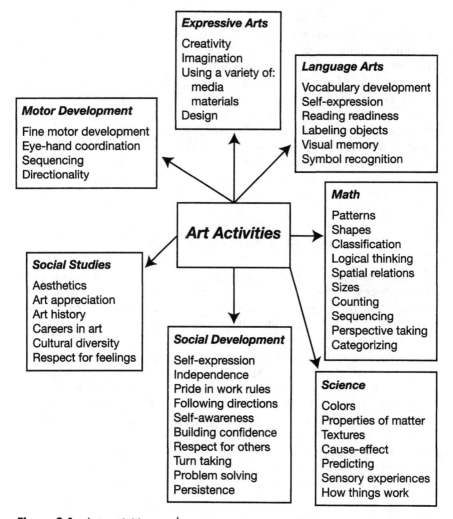

Figure 9.1. Art activities and assessment opportunities.

5. Preschematic drawing (5–7 years old)
6. Schematic stage (7–9 years old).

These stages of drawing development disclose a number of things about the children. Their conceptualization of the world around them is often represented through their artwork. Their use of form, perspective taking, and color are all mirrored in their art. And, less obviously, children's representational thinking ability and understanding of part-whole relationships are also reflected.

From a more purely maturational perspective, one can tell much about children's fine motor ability from their artwork. Their ability to grasp, to make steady, controlled marks, and to make coordinated figures are all areas that can be informally evaluated in the art area. Examples of their artwork are often included in children's portfolios as evidence of developmental progress. Children like to talk about their artwork, which provides teachers with a good opportunity to observe spontaneous language ability. Art in the curriculum can do much to enhance children's critical thinking, creative thinking, and aesthetic thinking as well as increase their awareness of the world around them (Althouse, Johnson, & Mitchell, 2003).

MUSIC AND MOVEMENT ACTIVITIES

Music and movement is a very natural as well as an important part of young children's development. Positive experiences in music and movement will enhance the child's intellectual development through creative expression, rhythmic movement, and listening. In addition, music experiences also build a foundation for later music appreciation.

According to the National Association for Music Education (1991), early music and movement experiences should be developmentally appropriate and involve singing, moving, and listening, as well as responding to visual and verbal representations of sounds. These activities give children the much needed experiences in associating symbols with their concrete referents. Music and movement does much to enhance children's critical thinking abilities through a creative and enjoyable process. Music and movement in the early childhood curriculum can do much to enhance all areas of development and learning (see Figure 9.2).

BLOCK ACTIVITIES

It is unfortunate that the use of blocks in the early childhood curriculum is seldom extended past kindergarten. Children learn much by using blocks, and teachers learn much about children by observing them use the blocks. As shown in Figure 9.3, children demonstrate a number of conceptual skills in their use of blocks:

- *Classification.* Using blocks of similar sizes and shapes for building a structure, for sorting the blocks in cooperative building, and for putting the blocks away on shelves

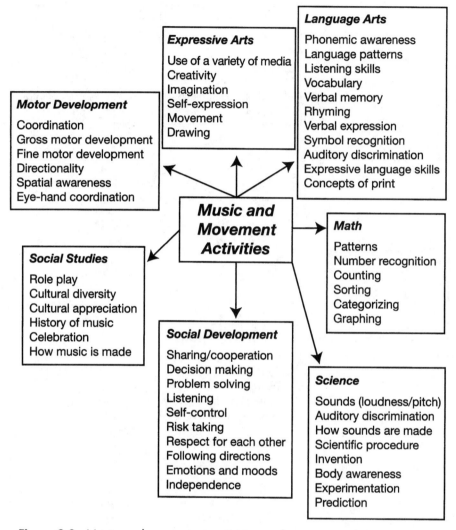

Figure 9.2. Music and movement activities and assessment opportunities.

- *Concepts.* Understanding or lack of understanding of size, shape, equivalency, one-to-one correspondence, seriation, measurement, and number; understanding figure-ground relationships and part-whole relationships
- *Language.* Expressing the names of the shapes and sizes and describing their constructions as they build using both attributional and functional vocabulary

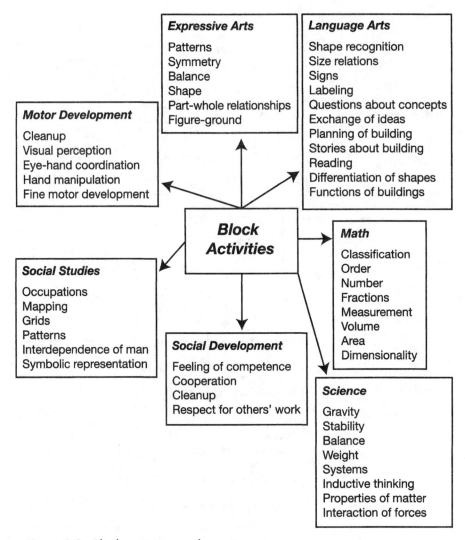

Figure 9.3. Block activities and assessment.

- *Sensorimotor skills.* Demonstrating balance, fine motor manipulation of objects, and perspective taking
- *Problem solving.* Negotiating with others, conserving, establishing equivalent sets using nonequivalent sizes of blocks, making storage decisions, and constructing geometric figures

DRAMATIC PLAY ACTIVITIES

Dramatic play can occur in a number of different classroom areas. The housekeeping corner of the room is most often associated with dramatic play. In addition, the puppet stage area and at times the rug and outside areas also facilitate dramatic play in young children. Dramatic play is rich in information regarding developmental and academic accomplishments (see Figure 9.4).

Language Development

Many insights about children's language development can be learned from observing them in dramatic play situations. Technical aspects of their language production, such as sentence structure and phonological development, become evident during spontaneous dramatic play. During dramatic play children may be less inhibited and therefore more likely to demonstrate their language capabilities. And the words children use in their spontaneous language during dramatic play is a good indication of the kinds of vocabulary skills they possess.

Social and Emotional Development

Dramatic play gives teachers an opportunity to evaluate children's abilities to relate to other children. Dramatic play situations often include some amount of cooperation and role play, and through these elements it is possible to determine particular aspects of the child's social development. Children often assume the roles of others, such as fathers, mothers, teachers, community helpers, or other children. Through these actions, it is possible to assess children's perceptions of others' social roles.

During dramatic play children's emotions may surface. Through the role play children often allow their fear, anger, joy, apprehension, excitement, or frustration to emerge during the themes that are played out. In early childhood education it is particularly important to understand how these emotions affect the day-to-day lives of children, including how they affect behavior in early education settings.

Concept and Skill Development

Dramatic play provides a nonthreatening vehicle that children can use to practice the skills and concepts they are acquiring. Through focused observation of children during these situations, teachers often can determine the extent to which the children have mastered the particular skills and concepts that are the focus of the curriculum objectives.

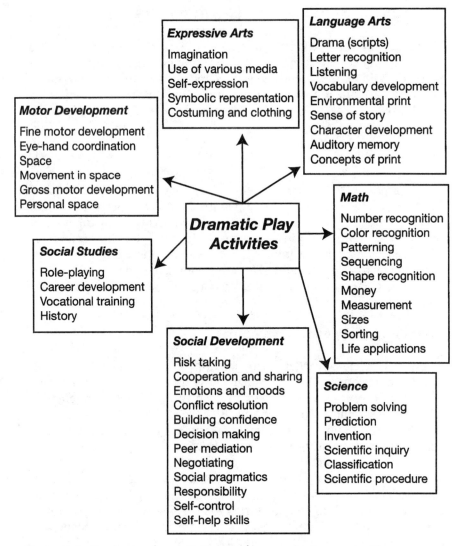

Figure 9.4. Dramatic play activities and assessment opportunities.

SCIENCE AND DISCOVERY ACTIVITIES

The science and discovery area in the early childhood classroom provides the principle location where teachers can observe children processing information, constructing new knowledge, reconstructing existing knowledge, and solving problems (see Figure 9.5). Through the kinds of activities that occur in the science and discovery area, children's understanding of

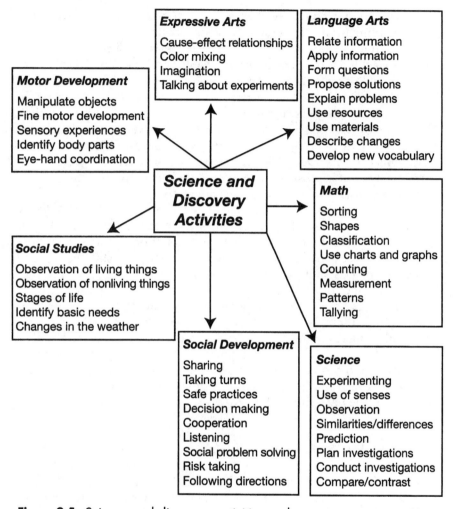

Figure 9.5. Science and discovery activities and assessment opportunities.

many early scientific principles can be evaluated. It should be noted that sand and water activity could also be included here.

Children's understanding of the process of transformation is one of the scientific principles that can be assessed. Do children understand whether or not a transformation is relevant? This is the primary requisite to the development of conservation concepts. A transformation is relevant if something has been added or subtracted from the original quantity. If the quantity has been changed perceptually, but nothing has been added to or taken from the quantity, the transformation is irrelevant. This understanding is important for certain problem-solving tasks.

Children's metacognitive ability can be assessed during science and discovery activities. Metacognition is awareness of one's own lack of understanding (Markman, 1977), not an easy task for the preoperational child who exhibits egocentric tendencies. Yet this is an important ability to possess in order to progress cognitively. Children's divergent thinking abilities can also be assessed through science activities. Divergent thinking refers to the ability to come up with multiple strategies for solving problems (Clements & Gullo, 1984). By observing children actively engaged in scientific activity, it is possible to determine the creativity that children use in their approach to problem-solving situations.

Teachers can learn much about children's attributional knowledge by observing them during discovery activities. Attributional knowledge means children's understanding of the characteristics of objects and how those properties affect their function. As teachers watch how children use and categorize objects spontaneously, children's understanding of object attributes becomes more obvious.

Finally, in addition to observing and assessing those general cognitive abilities discussed above, teachers can also observe and assess for children's understanding of specific knowledge. For example, if the class is engaged in a science unit on magnets, can children develop rules for what kinds of objects magnets can and cannot attract? In a unit on floating and sinking, can the children successfully categorize objects according to whether they can sink or float?

MATH AND MANIPULATIVES ACTIVITIES

Activities in the classroom's math and manipulatives areas can also be very informative regarding children's problem-solving skills. By manipulating different types of objects such as unifix cubes, pattern blocks, puzzles, and dice, children indicate their ability to sustain patterns, seriate (put objects in order), form geometric shapes, and perform mathematical operations.

In addition, there are also specialized mathematically oriented materials that may be available in some classrooms. As children manipulate cuisenaire rods, for example, teachers can observe their ability to estimate, demonstrate fractional relationships, and understand place value. By having opportunities to watch children manipulate Dienes Multibase Arithmetic Blocks, teachers will have a better basis for evaluating children's understanding of place value, regrouping, addition, and subtraction (Van de Walle, 2004).

By observing children using puzzles, teachers can learn about children's understanding of part-whole relationships. Children's visual discrimination of form may also be assessed to some extent.

Finally, children's fine motor abilities may be ascertained by observing their activity at the manipulatives or math areas. By discerning this, a teacher would be better able to make decisions regarding what type of objects are best suited for an individual child. Figure 9.6 indicates the range of skills and development that can be assessed through math and manipulatives activities.

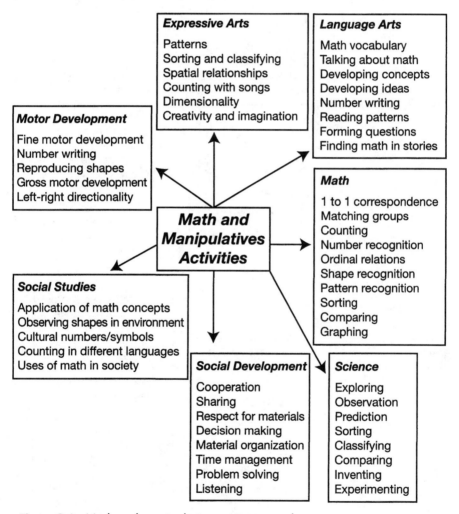

Figure 9.6. Math and manipulatives activities and assessment opportunities.

LITERACY ACTIVITIES

Today, early childhood education practitioners consider speaking, listening, reading, and writing to be integrated skills and developmental processes, and usually label them literacy. In early childhood, literacy develops through oral language and story (Fields, Groth, & Spangler, 2004). Teachers can tell much about children's language by noting their behavior in the literacy areas as well as other areas of the classroom (see Figure 9.7). In

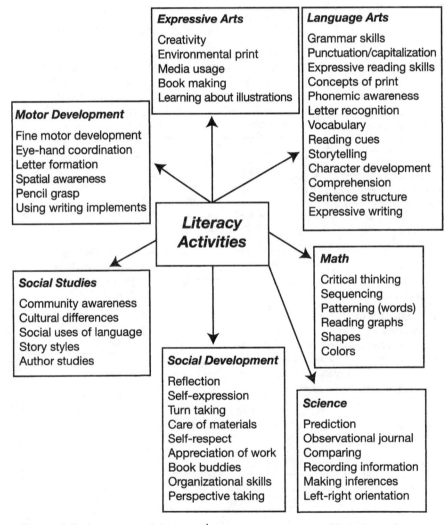

Figure 9.7. Literacy activities and assessment opportunities.

today's political climate, children are assessed regularly using standardized assessments in order to determine what specific skills they have acquired related to reading and writing, but teachers can also observe children
in the process of communication, either written or oral, to help understand how the process of reading and writing functions within the classroom context. Evaluating children's reading and writing skills, such as
sound-letter correspondence, sound analysis, decoding, spelling, listening,
and comprehension, are all possible by observing children in the literacy
and other areas of the classroom. During literature time teachers have
opportunities to assess children's capacity to tell or retell stories by focusing
on their capability to sequence events, recall details, demonstrate comprehension, and provide sufficient information so that others can understand
the story. As children get older, appraising children's writing can assess
similar capacities.

PART IV

Assessment and Evaluation with Special Populations of Children

CHAPTER 10

Understanding Assessment and Evaluation for Children with Special Needs

AS WAS DISCUSSED in Chapter 1, federal legislation regarding educational planning for children with special needs played an important role in shaping the assessment practices for early childhood education. While many of the principles that have been discussed in this book regarding the assessment of young children also apply to children with special needs, there are some differences. Many of these differences are mandated through the laws that guide the identification of and planning for children who are identified as having special educational needs.

There are many categories of special needs, and a discussion of each of these is beyond the scope of this book (for a thorough description of these categories, see Cohen & Spenciner, 2003). The range of special needs is wide in type and severity as they relate to children's ability to benefit from regular educational practices. In many situations, assessment will lead to special programming. The type of special need can range from a minor speech or language problem to something more debilitating such as a severe physical condition or cognitive delay. Also, children can be identified as having only one area of special need or multiples areas in need of remediation and/or special education services. All of these factors will determine the type or types of assessments that are used, the types of specialists that will become involved in the assessment process, and ultimately the kind or kinds of intervention programming that is suggested.

The primary purpose of the assessment procedure and subsequent programming related to the identification and planning for children with special needs focuses on four goals. As will be seen, not all the goals are realistic for all children who are identified.

The first goal is the amelioration of the disability. This goal may not be actualized for all children. For example, if a child is identified as having a speech or language problem, the speech pathologist may, through speech/language therapy, improve the child's capacity in speech and language so that he or she may no longer require special services. However, if a child is identified as having a physical or cognitive problem that is congenital, such a child will probably continue with special services throughout his or her schooling.

The second goal is the prevention of secondary disabling conditions. If, for example, a child's primary disability is in the physical domain, this could lead to cognitive or language delays if appropriate intervention is not pursued. This may also be true among children who have sensorial disabilities, such as deafness or blindness. It should be noted that some of these primary conditions might also lead to emotional or social problems as well. In assessing children, the goal is to identify the extent of the child's needs so that secondary disabling conditions can be lessened or avoided altogether.

The third goal is to support the needs of families of the children who are identified as having special needs. This also can vary in terms of what is required to support the family. If the child's program is greatly altered from what is considered a regular education program, families need to be kept apprised of what kinds of modifications will be made and the reasons for doing these modifications in the manner in which they are designed and executed. In addition, many children with special needs require continued support at home to maximize the benefits of the school program. Also, many families have questions about their child once he or she is identified as having special educational needs. The team of specialists, including the classroom teacher, should be sensitive to these family needs and respond accordingly, using assessment data whenever appropriate to substantiate what is conveyed to families.

Finally, the fourth goal is the design and implementation of unique curriculum and instruction strategies. The assessment information should give the professionals working with the child in school information as to what kinds of special modifications, if any, are required to support the child. Even children who are included in the regular classroom often require special modifications to the curriculum and instruction that is carried out in the classroom.

The remainder of this chapter will focus on two areas. In the next section, assessment as a decision-making process will be discussed. Although many of the assessment procedures used in general also apply for children with special needs, special applications of assessment will be described and discussed. In the second section of this chapter, suggestions will be offered and discussed related to using assessment information for the planning of curriculum and instruction.

In these discussions the emphasis will be on how assessment and evaluation are used in programming for the child with special needs. The focus will not be on how to develop programs themselves. For more information in developing programs for young children with special needs, the reader is referred to the following resources:

Including Children with Special Needs in Early Childhood Programs (Wolery & Wilbers, Eds., 1994)

Reaching Potentials: Appropriate Curriculum and Assessment for Young Children (Bredekamp & Rosegrant, Eds., 1992)

Children with Special Needs: Lessons for Early Childhood Professionals (Kostelnik, Onaga, Rohde, & Whiren, 2002)

Assessment of Children and Youth with Special Needs (Cohen & Spenciner, 2003)

ASSESSMENT AS A DECISION-MAKING PROCESS

According to Wolery, Strain, and Bailey (1992), there are seven decision points related to the process of assessment and the special needs child. It should be noted here that the process of assessment includes not only the implementation of assessment but also the use of the information that results from its implementation. Wolery et al. also list relevant questions to ask at each decision point (all page numbers in this section are from this source).

The first decision point is to determine whether or not to refer a child for special needs services and additional assessment. The type of assessment that is used in this situation is a screening assessment tool (see Chapter 4 for a discussion of screening assessments). According to Wolery et al. (1992), three relevant questions should be asked about the screening outcome:

- Does developmental screening indicate potential for developmental delay or disability?
- Does hearing or visual screening indicate potential sensory impairments or losses?
- Does health screening and physical examination indicate need for medical attention? (p. 98)

As can be seen from these questions, there are multiple reasons why children could be screened including possible developmental disabilities, sensory impairments, and health problems. Any or all of these three factors have the potential of affecting the child's educational plan and ultimately his or her educational experience.

The second decision point is to determine whether in fact the child, who has been referred as a result of the screening, has a developmental delay, sensory disability, or health-related problem. The type of assessment used to determine this is a diagnostic instrument (see Chapter 4 for a discussion of diagnostic instrumentation). The following questions should be asked after diagnostic assessment:

- Does a developmental delay or disability exist?
- If so, what is the nature and extent of the delay or disability? (p. 98)

These questions will help early childhood professionals determine not only whether or not a condition exists that may require special services, but also the severity of it if it does exist. It will also indicate whether there are multiple conditions present that may require different types of interventions from different types of specialists.

The third decision point is to determine from the diagnostic assessment whether or not the child is eligible for special education services. The child's diagnosis must be matched with the stated eligible conditions under which children can receive special education services. The following question should be asked:

- Does the child meet the criteria specified by the state to receive specialized services? (p. 98)

Once the child has been determined eligible for receiving special services, the fourth decision point is determining how the child should be taught within the program—instructional program planning assessment. There are a number of questions to be asked related to this decision point and related to assessment:

- What is the child's current level of developmental functioning?
- What does the child need to be independent in the classroom, home, and community?
- What are the effects of adaptations and assistance on the child's performance?
- What usual patterns of responding and what relationships with environmental variables appear to influence the child's performance? (p. 98)

The fifth decision point is used to determine where the child should receive the special education services and specifically what types of services are needed. In this situation, assessment information is used to make decisions related to placement. The following questions should be asked related to placement:

- What does the child need?
- Which of the possible placement options could best meet the child's needs?
- Does the child need specialized services, such as speech/language therapy, physical therapy, occupational therapy, or dietary supervision? (p. 98)

It should be noted that specialized services, such as those described above, may be the only indicated service needed or might be combined with other more general services related to the child's general educational needs. As stated earlier, many children receive multiple services.

The sixth decision point is determining whether or not the child is making appropriate progress in achieving those skills that are indicated in their Individual Educational Plan (IEP). The type of assessment that is used to determine this is a formative evaluation. Assessment of the child is implemented on a regular basis to determine progress and to suggest modifications that need to be made to insure progress. The question associated with this is:

- What is the child's usual performance of important skills? (p. 98)

Finally, the seventh decision point is to determine whether or not or to what extent the desired educational outcomes are being achieved. Program evaluation of a summative nature is used to determine this. The answers to the two following questions are looked for in the assessment data:

- Is the child using important skills outside the classroom?
- Did the child make expected progress? (p. 98)

To summarize, assessment and evaluation information should be used to make decisions regarding the following matters:

- Whether or not the child has a special educational need
- Whether or not the child is eligible for special services
- The type of special educational services that are best suited for the educational needs of the child
- The effectiveness of the services provided in the short term as well as the overall effectiveness of his or her program towards meeting the IEP goals

USING ASSESSMENT TO PLAN FOR CURRICULUM AND INSTRUCTION FOR THE CHILD WITH SPECIAL NEEDS

In addition to using assessment information in the decision making outlined above, it should be used effectively in planning for curriculum and instruction for a child who has been identified as needing special education services. While assessment is important in planning curriculum and instruction for all children, there are particular differences in how assessment is used for this purpose regarding a child with special needs.

Children who are identified as having special educational needs are in varied programs. Whenever possible, children are included in regular classrooms for the whole day or for part of the day. In full inclusion classrooms, children with special needs are integrated into the regular classroom. In other situations, some children with special needs may be in self-contained programs, if their needs are too many or too great for them to be included in a regular classroom. Regardless of how the child with special needs is educated, there are common attributes of curriculum and instruction that must be addressed, and in most cases, addressed through interpretation of assessment information. Assessment information should be used to determine the following:

- What kinds of curricular or instructional modifications need to be made in order to meet the specialized needs of the child.
- What kinds of environmental supports are required in the physical classroom space so that the educational experience of the child can be maximized.
- What kinds of adaptations are required in the materials that the child uses during the course of instruction.
- Whether or not there needs to be some sort of simplification of activities so that instructional goals can be met.
- What kinds of preferences the child has regarding general interests or optimal modes of learning, to name two examples. These preferences, once known should be used in the context of instruction in order to maximize learning opportunities. This is important for all young children, but essential for young children with special needs.
- What kinds of adult or peer support are required. If the child is in an inclusive classroom or mainstreamed for part or all of the day, it is imperative that peer support be given particular consideration (see Kemple, 2004).
- What kinds of specialized instruction might be required for the child with special needs. This may mean, for example, that shorter, but more frequent, activities are required in order to increase learning opportunities or opportunities for instruction (Azrin & Armstrong, 1973), or it may mean adjusting the activities or classroom routines by changing what children do in them (Wolery, 1994).

When assessment is used to plan for instruction, there are five characteristics of assessment that should be kept in mind (Wolery et al., 1992;

quoted characteristics are from this source). Although these characteristics are also pertinent to assessment and curriculum planning for all children, the manner in which these characteristics become actualized for the child with special needs is focused somewhat differently.

The first characteristic is that "assessment should include a variety of measures in a variety of settings" (p. 100). That is, different assessments should be used, such as criterion-referenced, curriculum-based, teacher-made tests, and the child should be assessed in different settings including at school and at home. In addition, interviews with people who know the child should also be conducted as part of the assessment process.

Second, "assessment results should provide a detailed description of the child's functioning" (p. 100). The data resulting from assessment should give information regarding these factors:

- Developmental levels among all areas that are relevant for that child and for his or her particular situation
- Indications of what the child is capable of doing and also what the child is not capable of doing, generally and within an educational setting
- Whether or not there are any external or internal factors that might affect or influence the child's skills or abilities

Third, "assessment activities should involve the child's family" (p. 100). The family should be involved in a number of ways, including the following:

- Receiving assessment information from those professionals that are appropriate to interpret the information to them
- Having opportunities to observe their child while he or she is being assessed so that they can better understand the assessment process and so that they will have firsthand observational knowledge about their child's performance on the assessments
- Being provided with information regarding their child's levels of development and resulting educational or health needs
- Having opportunities to gather additional information in order to validate the findings of the assessment process

Fourth, "assessment activities should be conducted by professionals from different disciplines" (p. 100). How many and what kinds of professionals should be included in the assessment process will depend solely on the nature of the suspected special need. This is also true regarding the frequency with which the child is reassessed. For some children, only one type of professional may be required to assess the child, but in more complex situations, additional professionals may assess the child. These might include a speech and language pathologist or audiologist, physical therapist, occupational therapist, social worker, medical professional, psychologist, and special education and regular education teacher.

Fifth and finally, "assessment activities should result in a list of high-priority objectives" (p. 100). For some children who have multiple needs, educational priorities should be determined in order to plan for effective instruction. In some situations, one particular special need will have to improve or be ameliorated before others will benefit from intervention. For example, if a child is identified as having an attention deficit disorder and also an auditory processing difficulty, a behavioral plan to lessen the effects of the attention deficit may have to be initially undertaken before any intervention can proceed with auditory processing.

The assessment process will often identify the need for many more academic or developmental skills than it is possible to teach the child in a given period of time. Thus the importance of prioritization becomes paramount. It is important that everyone who is involved with the child be involved in this prioritization process, including the child's family. Three criteria should be considered in prioritizing:

- Which skills will be most useful for the child?
- Which skills will have the most long-term benefits for the child?
- Which skills are deemed most important to the family?

In the above section, it was emphasized that assessment information not only be used to identify children with special needs, but once identified, information from assessment procedures should be used to plan for effective curriculum and instruction. It is important to note that there are many similarities in using assessment for children with special needs and those who are typically developing. The important point to remember is that assessment informs instruction.

A WORD OF CAUTION

While the assessment process is very useful for the identification of and educational planning for children with special needs, a word of caution is necessary regarding the use of assessment with very young children. While one of the primary foci of this book has been caution with young children and assessment, increased caution is necessary in this situation.

Concerns have been expressed by the Division for Early Childhood of the Council for Exceptional Children (2000), as well as other professional organizations including the National Association for the Education of

Young Children (2003), regarding assessment and young children with special needs. Three concerns have been expressed:

1. The potential exists that labeling children too early as having special needs will be detrimental for those children and their ability to reach their potential.
2. There is a lack of adequate assessment instruments for young children that are valid and reliable measures.
3. There is a belief that some of the categories used to describe a young child's disability, which are also used to describe the special needs of older children, may not be appropriate for younger children.

As a direct result of this third concern, states are permitted to use the term *developmental delay* when referring to children between the ages of 3 and 9 so that they can receive the necessary services without being specifically labeled. According to Cohen and Spenciner (2003), a developmental delay refers to a delay in one or more areas within the developmental domains of physical development, cognitive development, language development, social-emotional development, or adaptive development. Because all children vary in their levels of development, even if they are of the same age, it should be emphasized that a developmental delay refers to

> a condition which represents a significant delay in the process of development. It does not refer to a condition in which a child is slightly or momentarily lagging in development. The presence of a developmental delay is an indication that the process of development is significantly affected and that without special intervention, it is likely that educational performance at school age will be affected. (McLean, Smith, McCormick, Schakel, & McEvoy, 1991, p. 2)

In this chapter, a number of specific issues related to assessing children with special needs have been discussed with a focus on the purposes for assessment, along with how assessment is used for program development. In Chapter 11, similar assessment issues will be discussed for children who have culturally and linguistically diverse backgrounds.

Children with Culturally and Linguistically Different Backgrounds: Assessment and Evaluation Issues

C HILDREN WHO are receiving early childhood services are becoming increasingly diverse. According to the National Center for Education Statistics (2002), whites (non-Hispanic) comprise 63.5% of public school enrollment, with blacks (non-Hispanic) accounting for 17%, Hispanics for 14.4%, Asians/Pacific Islanders for 3.9%, and American Indian/Alaskan natives for 1.2%. This increase in the number of young children who are culturally or linguistically diverse has resulted in many challenges for early childhood educators. How to assess this growing population of children is in the forefront of these challenges. Identifying children who are eligible for special education programs is of special concern. Yansen and Shulman (1996) report that the number of children from culturally or linguistically diverse backgrounds who are referred to special education is much higher than would be expected from the population in general. This potentially reflects an error in the assessment process.

On the other hand, it is possible that there are a number of children from culturally or linguistically diverse backgrounds who go unidentified as in need of special services (McLean, 2000). It is suspected that this may be due to the difficulty of distinguishing between special needs and behaviors that reflect differences in culture. Therefore, assessment procedures must be carefully scrutinized in order to determine whether or not cultural biases exist that have the potential of leading to either overidentification or underidentification of children who may have special education needs and who come from homes that are culturally or linguistically different from the mainstream culture.

ASSESSMENT OF CHILDREN WITH CULTURAL
AND/OR LINGUISTIC DIFFERENCES

"Children's backgrounds have a profound influence on their knowledge, vocabulary, and skills" (McAfee & Leong, 2002, p. 19). While this statement is an important one for all children, especially when attempting to assess their knowledge and skills, it has particular significance for those young children who come from backgrounds that are culturally or linguistically different from those of children in the mainstream culture. If the goal of education is for all children to reach their optimal potential, then it is necessary that assessment of all children be fair and authentic regardless of their cultural, socioeconomic, or linguistic backgrounds (Committee for Economic Development, 1991). According to Neisworth and Bagnato (1996), most assessment practices are probably not appropriate for these groups of children. In addition to those issues related to the development of young children that render many assessment procedures not valid or reliable, there are additional issues that must be taken into account when assessing young children who come from culturally or linguistically diverse backgrounds.

In order to achieve valid and reliable assessment results that are not biased by the cultural or linguistic diversity of the child, careful selection of assessment instrumentation and procedures is necessary (McLean, 1998; Schiff-Meyers, 1992). In short, assessment procedures for this population of young children need to be different. Of course, many of the recommendations for assessing children who are culturally or linguistically diverse are the same as those for young children whose primary language is English and who come from the dominant culture. These include assessing the child in multiple settings using multiple measures, assessing the child in familiar contexts and natural settings, and involving the family in the assessment process and decision-making process. However, there are some distinct differences in assessing these two groups of children.

One of the most important considerations in deciding what kind of assessment instrument to use or what kinds of assessment procedures to utilize, is whether or not the instruments or procedures are sensitive to cultural differences. That is, do the instruments or procedures have built in safeguards so that it is possible to distinguish the difference between the impact of cultural and linguistic diversity on the child's development and learning and the presence of a learning difficulty or developmental delay (McLean, 2000)? This should become the overarching consideration when assessing children who are culturally or linguistically diverse.

The Division of Early Childhood of the Council for Exceptional Children recommends that three additional practices be added to the assessment procedure when assessing children who come from backgrounds that are culturally or linguistically diverse (reported in McLean, 2000):

1. Prior to assessment, professionals gather information in order to determine whether a child should be referred for assessment for special education or whether a child's patterns of development and behavior can be explained by language or cultural differences.
2. Appropriate procedures are followed to determine which language should be used in assessing the child and to understand the impact of second language acquisition on the child's development and performance in the early childhood setting.
3. Appropriate assessment strategies are tailored to the individual child and family when culturally appropriate and nonbiased instruments cannot be identified. (pp. 2–3)

For children whose language dominance is not English, information about the language dominance and language proficiency of the family needs to be understood. If it is determined that the family's language dominance and proficiency is other than English, an appropriate translator should be identified so that communication with the family can be facilitated.

It is more usual than not that a child interacts on a daily basis with other caregivers and other children who are not part of the child's immediate family, so it is important to have a clear understanding of the language dominance and proficiency of those individuals as well. These individuals have an important influence on the child, and an understanding of this influence may prove useful in understanding the assessment results or may suggest particular assessment procedures.

The family of the child should be involved in the assessment process in a number of ways. The family should be interviewed in order to get information on their impressions of their child's development. Ways in which different cultures use language for various situations is different, and getting specific information from families regarding these differences will be useful. After consulting with the child's family and getting their permission, others with whom the child comes in contact during the course of the day should also be interviewed to get their impressions of the child's development. Children, particularly young children, exhibit different behaviors in different contexts, and this will be useful information for the assessor.

In most instances, those who are assessing the child and making decisions regarding the educational services for which the child is qualified do not share the child's cultural background. Thus a *cultural guide* should be consulted to help interpret the child's behaviors. A cultural guide is an individual who is part of the child's culture and who is also knowledgeable about the mainstream culture. According to Gonzalez-Mena (1997):

People have individual values, personal inclinations, and behavior styles that determine how they will act. Any statement about culture is a generalization and doesn't tell you how an individual in that culture will act. You can see trends, themes, and probabilities, but be careful about generalizing that information to individuals. (p. 98)

Another additional measure that must be taken is screening the child for language dominance and proficiency. Then developmental screening should be done (in that language, if possible) for all of the other developmental domains—cognitive, social, emotional, motor, vision, and hearing.

Before the child is assessed, it is important that he or she have sufficient time to become accustomed to the early childhood setting's linguistic and cultural environment. All children need to have a level of comfort with their environment in order to obtain valid and useful assessment data, but this is of special significance for those children whose language or cultural background is different from the majority of those in that setting. In addition, the child should be observed both at home as well as in the early childhood school setting.

Finally, and of utmost importance, the child who is linguistically diverse should be observed and assessed in settings where language is not required, neither comprehension or expression of language. Many assessments, especially early childhood assessments require a certain level of language proficiency, even when assessing those developmental domains or academic skills that are not language related. In these cases, if the child is not proficient in English, even the results of the assessment for developmental or academic areas other than the language-related area are influenced by the child's abilities to use and understand language.

> In summary, the assessment of young children with culturally and linguistically different backgrounds cannot be "business as usual." Considerable information from the child and family should be obtained and considered prior to the initial referral for assessment. The assessment team must then make every effort to tailor the assessment so it becomes appropriate for the individual child and family. Efforts to provide a culturally and linguistically appropriate assessment will help to guard against over- or underidentification of children for special education services. (McLean, 1998, p. 25)

An additional factor that is often overlooked or not considered is the background of the teacher or other professionals who work with children in the capacity of teaching or assessment. The early childhood professionals who are responsible for the care, teaching, or assessment of young children have to recognize that they too are the products of their own social and cultural backgrounds. As a result, they often have little intentional knowledge of why they act the way they do, why they have the values that they have, and why they have certain expectations of others. A potential problem exists when they judge others' behaviors based upon their own cultural or social standards (McAfee & Leong, 2002). According to Guerin and Maier (1983), the cultural characteristics that are most relevant to school and are often subject to misinterpretation by those who are not from the same social or cultural group include learning styles, interpersonal relationships between children and adults, attitudes toward school achievement, and style of behaving. This misinterpretation may lead to unnecessarily referring a child to be assessed for special needs, or not fully understanding what skills and knowledge the child is capable of.

NONBIASED ASSESSMENT INSTRUMENTS AND STRATEGIES FOR CHILDREN WITH CULTURAL AND LINGUISTIC DIFFERENCES

One of the foremost challenges facing early childhood educators today is identifying assessment instruments and procedures that are bias free. Valencia and Suzuki (2001) argue for a judicious use of a variety of assessment instruments and strategies in such a manner that cultural diversity can be both included and used to demonstrate competence. If this is done, only then can schools achieve what has been called *multicultural validity* (Kirkhart, 1995). In considering multicultural validity in the development of assessments, the assessor must keep in mind how cultural diversity might influence the following factors:

- The manner in which the assessment data are collected
- The reliability of the match between the assessment instrument or procedure and the individual who is being assessed
- The consequences of how the results of the assessment are being applied to the individual who is being assessed

Designers of assessment instruments have found it nearly impossible to develop tests that are culture free and that can be used with equal confidence among all cultural and linguistic groups (Goodwin & Goodwin, 1993). As a result, developers of assessments have tried to include items in the test that do not favor one cultural group over another, do not favor one geographic area over another, and are not offensive or meaningless to particular groups (Wortham, 2001). These issues are particularly pertinent to the design and implementation of standardized measures of assessment.

In addition to the design of the test, there are also issues related to scoring and standardization. If the scoring procedures and standardization procedures were developed and based on a limited population (e.g., all white, middle-class children), the results of the assessment would not necessarily be applicable to children who come from culturally or linguistically different backgrounds. Even if the instrument were translated into the child's dominant language, if it were standardized on a cultural group other than that of the child's, the results might still not be valid or reliable, regardless of the language of implementation.

The Early Childhood Research Institute for Culturally and Linguistically Appropriate Services (CLAS) makes available many resources for early childhood professionals that offer suggestions, advice, and research so that informed decisions can be made relative to children who come from culturally and linguistically diverse backgrounds. Among the resources, CLAS provides information to early childhood educators, other professionals working with young children, policy makers, and families, to assist them in choosing assessments that are appropriate for the linguistic and cultural background of the child. "The goals of the CLAS Institute were to identify, evaluate, and promote effective and appropriate early intervention practices and preschool practices that are sensitive and respectful to children and families from culturally and linguistically diverse backgrounds" (Fowler, Santos, & Corso, 2004).

To assist early childhood professionals in making decisions about choosing assessments that are nonbiased for children who come from culturally or linguistically different backgrounds, CLAS developed four guidelines. The individual or individuals implementing the assessment will need to read the testing manual carefully to determine if the suggested guidelines have been addressed. It is important to note that even those assessment instruments that have involved children from diverse cultures and linguistic backgrounds may not be appropriate for a particular child (McLean, 2000). The most appropriate assessment is one that addresses the elements of the CLAS guidelines:

1. *Scoring procedure.* If the assessment procedure or instrument has a scoring or rating scale, it should be noted which types of cultural or linguistic groups were initially included in the development of these scoring scales. It should also be noted whether or not there are separate scoring or normative scales for the specific cultural or linguistic groups. Appropriate assessment instruments were developed involving different cultural or linguistic groups and have separate scoring scales for those groups.

2. *Incorporation of information from the specific culture into the assessment procedures.* Many assessments describe themselves as being appropriate for particular cultural or linguistic groups. If this is stated, it should then be noted whether or not information about parenting practices and child development that is typical for the specific cultural group is taken into account in the design and implementation of the assessment.

3. *Modifications of the assessment.* It should be noted in the examiner's manual whether or not there exists suggestions for modifying the assessment for children who come from culturally or linguistically different backgrounds. This is especially important for those instruments that are standardized to ensure that the modifications are standardized for these groups of children. Modification is potentially important in that it is known that not all cultural or linguistic groups behave in the same manner or respond in the same manner to questions and these differences in behaviors may yield inaccurate results if no modifications are suggested.

4. *Interpretation of the findings.* The early childhood professional whose responsibility it is to assess children should examine the assessment to determine if there are specific recommendations for interpreting the behaviors of children who are culturally or linguistically diverse.

If it is determined that the assessment tool that is being considered for use does not meet the characteristics of these guidelines, alternative assessment tools or procedures should be considered. Assessment tools or procedures that better meet the needs of culturally or linguistically diverse children should be sought out and ultimately used.

FINAL REMINDER

The assessment of young children who come from culturally or linguistically diverse backgrounds represents somewhat of a double-edged sword. First, one has to keep in mind the development of the child and all the limitations related to assessment that are relevant to the child's level of development. These include such things as cognitive, language, or motor limitations of the young child that may influence assessment results. In addition, given the fact that young children develop so quickly and developmental change is rapid, reliable and valid assessment results often are not easily obtained or, if obtained, are not useful for the purpose for which they were intended.

In addition, one also has to consider the cultural and linguistic background of the child. The experiences that children have as a result of coming from these diverse backgrounds may also influence the assessment findings. One has to take extreme care in choosing assessment instruments and procedures and interpreting the results for placement in special programs or for curriculum modification.

Epilogue

MAKING DECISIONS! Making decisions is one of the primary things that early childhood professionals do. They make decisions related to curriculum content and to curriculum implementation strategies. They make decisions related to which practice is best suited for which purpose and for which child. Most of the information that teachers base their decision making on is provided by the children themselves.

Assessment and evaluation are useful tools that can help collect, organize, and make sense out of the information that early childhood professionals gather about children and the curriculum. In a sense, all competent teachers are early childhood researchers: collecting data, generating knowledge, and defining and redefining practice based upon the information collected and the knowledge generated. Understanding assessment and evaluation, as well as the potential implications for their use, is the basis for making sound decisions. However, it is widely known in research that one can use the data in different ways, even to justify inappropriate practices. In today's accountability climate, these words were never truer. It is hoped that this book has shed some light on the role of assessment and evaluation in early childhood education in such a way as to enable practitioners to use the information they gather to make valid decisions about the status and future of the children in their charge. The decisions they make based upon this information greatly affect how children learn and how they live. Ultimately, there are few decisions of greater import to be made.

Selected Assessment Instruments in Early Childhood Education

IN THIS appendix, a number of assessments will be described. The instruments will be categorized as readiness tests, achievement tests, developmental screening tests, or diagnostic tests. This is not meant to be an exhaustive list of instruments found in the field nor is it meant to be an endorsement. The choice of instruments found in this appendix represents those that are most likely to be used or encountered by early childhood educators.

READINESS TESTS

Basic School Skills Inventory, 3rd ed. (BSSI-3)

D. Hammill, J. Leigh, N. Pearson, and T. Maddox, 1998, Austin, TX: Pro-Ed

The BSSI-3 is an assessment that is designed to be used by classroom teachers. It yields information that is directly related to the basic skills that are considered important for early school success. The BSSI-3 is appropriate for children between the ages of 4 and 8. The areas that are assessed include spoken language, reading, writing, math, classroom behavior, and daily living skills.

Boehm Test of Basic Concepts

A. E. Boehm, 1986, San Antonio, TX: Psychological Corporation

The Boehm Test is an individually or group-administered instrument. It was designed to be used with children between 3 and 5 years old. The test can be administered by teachers and assesses children's understanding of the following concepts: size, direction, special relationships, and quantity. The information derived from the test's scores can be used by the teacher as a guide for curriculum planning. It has also been viewed as a good measure of school readiness.

Brigance Diagnostic Inventory of Early Development—Revised

A. Brigance, 1991, North Billerica, MA: Curriculum Associates

This instrument is criterion referenced and designed to be used with children below the developmental level of 7 years. A variety of assessment methods are used, including parent interview and teacher observation. The goal of the assessment is to identify those segments of the curriculum objectives that have been mastered by children in the class. It can be used as an assessment instrument, instructional guide, and a record-keeping tracking system. The areas that are assessed include knowledge and comprehension, preacademics, psychomotor, self-help, and speech and language.

Cognitive Skills Assessment Battery (CSAB)

A. E. Boehm and B. R. Slater, 1981, New York: Teachers College Press

The CSAB is a criterion-referenced assessment instrument. It was designed to be used with children in prekindergarten and kindergarten. It can be given by teachers in the beginning of the school year to assist in curriculum planning. The CSAB assesses the child's environment, discrimination of similarities and differences, comprehension, concept formation, coordination, and memory.

Preschool Screening System (PSS)

P. Hainsworth and M. Hainsworth, 1994, Pautucket, RI: ERISys

The PSS is designed to be individually administered to children between the ages of 4 years, 4 months and 5 years, 4 months. The screening system when combined with the accompanying parent questionnaire can be used to better meet individual children's needs through curriculum development. The PSS gives a quick indication of learning skills. The parent questionnaire provides information regarding children's home behavior, medical history, and developmental information.

Test of Basic Experiences, 2nd ed. (TOBE-2)

M. Moss, 1979, Columbus, OH: McGraw-Hill

The TOBE-2 is an assessment that is appropriate for children who are between prekindergarten and first grade. The purpose of the test is to assess those concepts that are thought to be important for school readiness. Areas assessed include math, language, science, and social studies. The TOBE-2 is available in a prekindergarten-kindergarten form and a first-grade form.

ACHIEVEMENT TESTS

California Achievement Test, 5th ed. (CAT-5)

1992, Columbus, OH: CTB/McGraw-Hill

The CAT-5 is a group-administered, norm-referenced test. The intended purpose of the test is to provide information for making educational decisions regarding improved instruction in the basic skills. The content areas that are assessed include literacy, spelling, language, math, science, social studies, and study skills.

Comprehensive Test of Basic Skills, 4th ed.

1990, Columbus, OH: CTB/McGraw-Hill

This assessment is used to assess progress in basic skills in children from kindergarten through 12th grade. Areas assessed include reading and language, spelling, math, science, social studies, and study skills.

Iowa Test of Basic Skills (ITBS)

1990, Chicago: Riverside Publishing Company

The ITBS is both a criterion- and norm-referenced test and measures overall academic functioning rather than specific content assessment. Level 5 is for students who are in kindergarten through Grade 1.5 and measures vocabulary, listening, word analysis, language, and math. Level 8 is for students who are in Grades 2.5 to 3.5 and measures word analysis, vocabulary, reading comprehension, spelling, math concepts, math problem solving, and math computation.

Kaufmann Test of Educational Achievement (KTEA)

A. Kaufmann and N. Kaufmann, 1985, Circle Pines, MN: American Guidance Service

The KTEA is a norm-referenced test and assesses multiple skills. The results of the assessment can be used for both program planning and making placement decisions. The Brief Form is appropriate for screening, while the Comprehensive Form is for identifying both strengths and weaknesses in students.

Metropolitan Achievement Tests, 7th ed. (MAT-7)

G. A. Prescott, 1993, San Antonio, TX: Psychological Corporation

The MAT-7 is designed to provide a comprehensive assessment of the student's skill development in the following areas: reading, math, language, social studies, and science. The complete battery is appropriate for screening and monitoring group performance. It can also be used for program evaluation.

Stanford Early Achievement Test, 3rd ed.

1989, San Antonio, TX: Psychological Corporation

This assessment is group administered and deigned to measure cognitive abilities in young children. Level I is to be administered to children before they enter kindergarten and Level II is designed for children at the end of kindergarten and the beginning of first grade. Areas assessed are sounds and letters, reading words, listening to words and stories, math, and environment. According to the test manual, the results can provide information regarding an individual's cognitive development as a baseline for instructional planning. The test is norm referenced and can be administered by the teacher.

Wechsler Individual Achievement Test (WIAT-11)

D. Wechsler, 2001, San Antonio, TX: Psychological Corporation

The WIAT-11 is a comprehensive battery that measures basic reading, math reasoning, spelling, reading comprehension, number operations, listening comprehension, oral expression, and written expression. A shorter version is also available for the purposes of screening.

Wide Range Achievement Test, 3rd ed. (WRAT-3)

G. Wilkinson, 1993, Wilmington, DE: Jastak Associates

The WRAT-3 was designed to measure the codes needed to learn the basic skills of reading, spelling, and math. The design of the assessment is such that it eliminates the possible effects of comprehension. It can be used to assess learning ability in children.

Work Sampling System

S. J. Meisels, 2001, Upper Saddle River, NJ: Pearson Education

The Work Sampling System was designed as an alternative assessment system that utilizes three separate components: developmental checklists, portfolios, and summary reports. The assessments are taken from actual work done by children in the class along with teacher observation of children engaged in the learning process. Together, these elements are classroom focused and relevant to instruction.

DEVELOPMENTAL SCREENING TESTS

AGS Early Screening Profiles

P. Harrison, 1990, Circle Pines, MN: American Guidance Service

This screening instrument provides information on developmental screening and intervention planning for children between the ages of 2 and 6. Assessment of cognitive development, language development, motor development, social development, and self-help skills are included.

Child Development Inventory (CDI)

H. Ireton, 1992, Minneapolis: Behavior Science Systems

This assessment is appropriate for children between the ages of 15 months and 6 years. The CDI is a measure of the child's current levels of development according to parent report. The eight subscales include social development, self-help, gross motor, fine motor, expressive language, language comprehension, letters, and numbers. The child's developmental profile, along with strengths and problems are highlighted in the report.

Developmental Indicators for the Assessment of Learning, 3rd ed. (DIAL-3)

C. Mardell-Czudnowski and D. Goldenberg, 1998, Minneapolis, MN: American Guidance Service

The DIAL-3 is an individually administered screening instrument. It is meant to be used with children between 2 and 6 years old. The following developmental areas are assessed: motor skills, conceptual skills, self-help, social development, and language skills. Scaled scores are derived for each of the subtests as well as for the total score. The test can potentially identify children who are at risk for academic failure as well as those who are academically precocious.

Early Screening Inventory—Revised

S. J. Meisels, D. B. Marsden, M. S. Wiske, and L. Henderson, 1997, New York: Pearson Early Learning

The purpose of this screening instrument is to identify children who are at risk according to the areas identified by the Individuals with Disabilities Act. The domains assessed include cognition, communication, and motor development. Optional scales in social/emotional and adaptive behaviors are also available.

McCarthy Screening Test (MST)

D. McCarthy, 1980, San Antonio, TX: Psychological Corporation

The MST is an individually administered test that is made up of 6 of the 18 subtests of the McCarthy Scales of Children's Abilities. The following areas are assessed: right-left orientation, verbal memory, draw-a-design, numerical memory, conceptual grouping, and leg coordination. The scores are norm referenced by age. The test can be used with children between 4 and 6½ years old.

Minneapolis Preschool Screening Instrument (MPSI)

R. Lichtenstein, 1982, Minneapolis, MN: Minneapolis Public Schools

The MPSI assesses skills in a number of areas that are then combined to determine whether or not there is need for further diagnostic assessment. Areas assessed include building, copying shapes, information, matching, sentence completion, hopping and balancing, naming colors, prepositions, identifying body parts, and repeating sentences. The MPSI is appropriate for children between the ages of 3 years, 7 months and 5 years, 4 months.

Screening Assessment for Gifted Elementary Students—Primary (SAGES-P)

S. Johnson and A. Corn, 1992, Austin, TX: Pro-Ed

This screening assessment may be helpful in identifying gifted children in kindergarten through Grade 3. The subtests include both reasoning (a measure of aptitude) and general information (a measure of achievement).

DIAGNOSTIC TESTS

Battelle Developmental Inventory (BDI)

J. Newborg, J. Stock, L. Wnek, J. Guidubaldi, and J. Sninicki, 1984 (with norms recalibrated in 1988), Chicago: Riverside Publishing Company

The BDI is both a norm- and criterion-referenced diagnostic instrument. It is an appropriate test for children between the ages of birth and 8. The following domains are assessed: personal-social, language/communication, cognitive, adaptive, and motor development. The test must be administered by trained individuals. The BDI also includes instructions for administrations to children with physical handicaps.

Bayley Scales of Infant Development

N. Bayley, 1993, San Antonio, TX: Psychological Corporation

The Bayley is an individual assessment appropriate for measuring the developmental progress of children between the ages of birth and 2½. It contains a Mental Scale, Motor Scale, and Behavior Scale. The purpose of the Bayley is to identify potential developmental delays in very young children. Administration is by a highly trained individual.

Kaufman Assessment Battery for Children (KABC)

A. Kaufman and N. Kaufman, 1983, Circle Pines, MN: American Guidance Service

The KABC is a norm-referenced intelligence and achievement test. It is individually administered and appropriate for children between 2 and 15 years of age. The test is divided into three areas: sequential processing, simultaneous processing, and achievement. The KABC was designed for use in both clinical and academic settings.

McCarthy Scales of Children's Abilities (MSCA)

D. McCarthy, 1972, San Antonio, TX: Psychological Corporation

The MSCA is an individually administered, norm-referenced assessment instrument. It was designed for use with children between the ages of 2½ and 8½. It consists of 18 separate subtests, the scores of which are combined to assess six developmental domains: verbal, perceptual-performance, quantitative, general cognitive, memory, and motor. The test can be used to diagnose children with learning difficulties or other exceptional conditions.

Peabody Picture Vocabulary Test, 3rd ed. (PPVT-III)

L. Dunn and L. Dunn, 1997, Circle Pines, MN: American Guidance Service

The PPVT-III is an individually administered, norm-referenced test. It is designed for children 2½ years of age and older. It measures children's receptive vocabulary ability. Scores are provided in the form of standard scores, percentiles, age scores, and stanine scores. It is not intended for use as a substitute measure of cognitive functioning. This is especially true for children with disabilities.

Preschool Language Scale, 4th ed. (PLS-4)

T. Zimmerman, V. Steiner, and R. Pond, 1992, San Antonio, TX: Psychological Corporation

The PLS-4 is an individually administered test that is used to identify children who may have a language delay. It is designed for use with children between the ages of birth and 7. It contains both auditory comprehension and expressive communication subscales. The PLS-4 differs from earlier editions by the provision of new norms that are more closely aligned with IDEA legislation.

Test of Early Language Development, 3rd ed. (TELD-3)

W. Hresko, D. Reid, and D. Hammill, 1999, Austin, TX: Pro-Ed

The TELD-3 is an individually administered test appropriate for use with children between the ages of 2 and 7. The purpose of the TELD-3 is to identify children who are significantly language delayed as compared to their age peers, to assess their language strengths, and to document their progress as a result of intervention. The TELD-3 assesses both receptive and expressive language abilities.

Test of Language Development—Primary, 3rd ed. (TOLD-P3)

P. Newcomer and D. Hammill, 1997, Austin, TX: Pro-Ed

The TOLD-P3 is an individually administered assessment for children between the ages of 4 and 9. It is designed to identify children who are significantly below their age peers in language performance. It assesses listening, speaking, semantics, syntax, and phonology. Results can also be used to monitor children's progress during intervention.

Wechsler Preschool and Primary Scale of Intelligence, 3rd ed. (WPPSI-3)

D. Wechsler, 2002, San Antonio, TX: Psychological Corporation

The WPPSI-3 is a norm-referenced intelligence test designed for use with children between the ages of 3 and 7. The test includes a verbal scale and a performance scale. The test yields a Verbal IQ, Performance IQ, and a Full Scale IQ. Special training to administer the test is required in addition to a background in psychometric assessment procedures and knowledge of the effects of culture on performance.

Glossary of Assessment and Evaluation Terms

Accountability. The process of accepting responsibly for one's actions. Educational accountability is accepting responsibility for the appropriate education of all children.

Achievement test. Assessment used to determine children's mastery of curriculum content after a period of instruction.

Age-equivalent score. Indicates the average chronological age of children achieving a particular score on an assessment.

Alternative assessment. An assessment option that focuses on methods other than strict adherence to the standard tests and measurement paradigm.

Alternative-form reliability. A type of test reliability in which two alternative forms of an assessment are compared and is an indication that the two forms of the assessment can be used interchangeably.

Analytic rubric. A type of rubric that describes and scores each task attribute separately and can be used for diagnostic purposes.

Anecdotal records. Brief written notes describing significant events in a child's experiences during the school day.

Assessment. The process of gathering information about children in order to make educational decisions.

Authentic assessment. Alternative assessment.

Central tendency. A set of numbers that exemplify the typical score in a set of scores.

Checklists. Instruments used to record and examine sequenced series of behaviors or skills that are usually directly related to educational or developmental goals.

Comparative evaluation. A type of evaluation in which alternative program outcomes are compared.

Concurrent validity. A type of criterion-related validity that refers to the degree to which the score on a test is related to the score on a different but similar test.

159

Content standards. Refers to *what* should be learned within the various curriculum content areas.

Content validity. A measure of the extent to which an assessment's content is related to the intended purpose of the assessment.

Criterion-referenced test. An assessment that compares a child's performance in skills and knowledge to accepted levels.

Criterion-related validity. Evidence that the resulting scores on an assessment are related to one or more outcome criteria.

Culturally appropriate. Refers to the recognition that to some extent all assessments are a measure of the child's cultural experiences. The child's cultural background should be taken into account when determining assessment tools and procedures.

Current-year portfolio. A portfolio that contains the work that was mutually agreed upon by the teacher and the child that meet certain criteria.

Curriculum-based assessment. A wide-ranging approach to assessment that directly links the assessment process to the curriculum content and instructional strategies used within the classroom.

Developmental rubic. A rubric that can be used across age levels and focuses on the idea that mastery is a developmental process.

Diagnostic test. An assessment used to determine an individual child's educational and/or developmental strengths and weaknesses. The results from diagnostic tests are used to suggest educational planning.

Direct observation. A procedure for observing children during the course of a learning activity.

Dynamic assessment. A form of alternative assessment during which the learner is directly engaged in the learning process by using mediated learning experiences. This approach utilizes a test-intervene-retest paradigm.

Early childhood. The period of life between the ages of birth and age eight. In schools, early childhood includes prekindergarten through Grade 3.

Evaluation. The process of making judgments about the merit, value, or worth of educational programs, projects, materials, or techniques.

Event sampling. A type of anecdotal record that focuses on behaviors during a specific event, such as during recess or during large group time.

Formative evaluation. Ongoing evaluation used to measure program quality and focus on elements that can still be modified.

Generalizability. The degree to which an individual's knowledge or skills can be applied appropriately in a variety of contexts.

Grade-equivalent score. Indicates the average grade level at which a certain score on an assessment is achieved.

High-stakes testing. The practice of using any measurement for making life-affecting decisions that will affect the educational future of a child.

Holistic rubric. A type of rubric that yields a single score that is applied to a child's overall performance.

Individualized Educational Plan (IEP). The formal contract that describes the educational intervention determined appropriate for a child who has been identified as having special educational or developmental needs.

Integrated curriculum. Curriculum design in which each of the component parts is recognized individually for its significance, but each of the components is also recognized as part of a significant whole.

Linguistically appropriate. Refers to the recognition that to some extent all assessments are a measure of the child's language ability. The child's language background should be taken into account when determining assessment tools and procedures.

Mean. A measure of central tendency and represents the average score in a set of scores.

Measurement. Assessment.

Median. A measure of central tendency that represents the score in the middle of a distribution of scores.

Mode. A measure of central tendency that represents the most frequently occurring score in a distribution of scores.

Multicultural validity. A process whereby assessment strategies are used in such a manner that cultural diversity can be both included and used to demonstrate competence.

Noncomparative evaluation. A type of evaluation in which program outcomes are assessed within a single group.

Norm-referenced. Refers to assessment instruments that allow one to compare an individual child's score with those of other children of similar chronological age.

Percentile score. A measure of variability that indicates an individual child's ranking in the distribution of scores indicated by a comparison group. It indicates what percentage of the comparison group scored either higher or lower than the child.

Performance standards. The levels of achievement that are thought to be appropriate for individual grade levels.

Permanent portfolio. A portfolio that contains very selected work that will accompany the child to his or her next class.

Play-based assessment. A form of assessment that is based on the teacher's knowledge of a child's play to assess the child's developmental level and/or academic skills and knowledge.

Portfolio assessment. A type of assessment in which assessment information about children is organized in folders or boxes. Portfolios can include examples of children's work as well as standardized test performance.

Predictability. The degree to which a process can accurately estimate future performance.

Predictive validity. A type of criterion-related validity that is a measure of the stability of the test score over time.

Project assessment. Used to assess a child's academic progress through the assessment of their knowledge and problem-solving skills by observing them in actual problem-solving situations.

Psychometric. A measurement technique used to assess cognitive functioning.

Range. A measure of variability that represents the difference between the highest and lowest score in a distribution of scores.

Rating scales. Instruments used to describe the degree to which behaviors, traits, or skills are present in an individual child.

Raw score. The actual score that an individual attains on a given assessment measure.

Readiness. The child's ability to construct and reconstruct knowledge and skills in a way that is consistent with the expectations of the school and the formal curriculum.

Readiness test. Assessment used to measure the degree to which children are prepared for an academic or preacademic program.

Rubric. A quantitative measure applied to children's actual work for the purpose of assessment. A rubric is a set of guidelines that distinguish levels of quality between products or performances. A rubric contains descriptors of what to look for at each level of performance.

Running record. A type of anecdotal record that is a more detailed description of a sequence of behaviors, rather than a description of a single incident.

Screening test. An assessment used to determine whether or not a child may benefit from an alternative educational experience or require further diagnostic assessment.

Split-half reliability. A form of test reliability in which one half of the test is compared with the score on the second half of the test to determine internal consistency.

Standard deviation. A measure of variability that represents the average amount that a particular score deviates from the mean.

Standard score. A measure of variability that permits the comparison of a child's performance on one assessment to his or her score on another assessment.

Standardized test. A test that compares an individual's performance to that of others with similar characteristics.

Standards. Explicitly stated educational goals.

Summative evaluation. The process of gathering information to determine the worth of an overall instructional sequence so that decisions can be made whether to retain or adopt that sequence. Summative evaluation is done at the end of an educational sequence.

Test reliability. A measure of test consistency.

Test-retest reliability. A type of test reliability in which an assessment is given more than once over a period of time in order to determine whether or not the resulting scores are comparable.

Time sampling. An assessment used to determine the frequency of targeted behaviors.

Works-in-progress portfolio. A portfolio that contains the work that children are currently working on.

References

Airasian, P. W., & Madaus, G. F. (1983). Linking testing and instruction: Policy issues. *Journal of Educational Measurement, 20*(2), 103–108.

Align to Achieve. (2003). *The standards database.* Watertown, MA: Author. Available online: http://www.aligntoachieve.org/AchievePhaseII/basic-search.cfm

Althouse, R., Johnson, M., & Mitchell, S. (2003). *The colors of learning: Integrating the visual arts into the early childhood curriculum.* New York: Teachers College Press.

American Educational Research Association (AERA), American Psychological Association (APA), & National Council on Measurement in Education (NCME). (1999). *Standards for educational and psychological testing.* Washington, DC: American Psychological Association.

American Institutes of Research. (2003). *Program review instrument for systems monitoring (PRISM) manual.* Washington, DC: Author.

American Psychological Association (1974). *Standards for educational and psychological tests and manuals.* Washington, DC: Author.

Anastasiow, N. J. (1986). *Development and disability: A psychobiological analysis for special educators.* Baltimore: Brookes.

Apgar, V. (1953). Proposal for a new method of evaluating the newborn infant. *Anesthesia and Analgesia, 52,* 260–267.

Apple, M., & King, N. (1978). What do schools teach? In G. Willis (Ed.), *Qualitative education: Concepts and cases in curriculum criticism.* Berkeley, CA: McCrutchan.

Aschbacher, P. R. (2000, Winter). Developing indicators of classroom practice to monitor and support school reform. *CRESST Line,* pp. 6–8.

Azrin, N. H., & Armstrong, P. M. (1973). The "mini-meal": A method of teaching eating skills to the profoundly retarded. *Mental retardation, 11*(1), 9–13.

Bagnato, S. J., Neisworth, J. T., & Munson, S. M. (1989). *Linking developmental assessment and early intervention: Curriculum-based prescriptions.* Rockville, MD: Aspen.

Bell, M. (1972). *A study of the readiness room program in a small school district in suburban Detroit.* Unpublished doctoral dissertation, Wayne State University, Detroit, MI.

Benson, T. R., & Smith, L. J. (1998). Portfolios in first grade: Four teachers learn to use alternative assessment. *Early Childhood Education, 25*(3), 173–180.

Bergen, D. (1997). Using observational techniques for evaluating young children's learning. In O. Saracho & B. Spodek (Eds.), *Issues in early childhood educational assessment and evaluation* (pp. 108–128). New York: Teachers College Press.

Bergen, D., & Mosley-Howard, S. (1994). Assessment methods for culturally diverse young children. In D. Bergen (Ed.), *Assessment methods for infants and toddlers: Transdisciplinary team approaches* (pp. 190–206). New York: Teachers College Press.

Blank, M., & Allen, D. (1976). Understanding "why." In M. Lewis (Ed.), *Origins of intelligence: Infancy and early childhood* (pp. 259–278). New York: Plenum Press.

Bodrova, E., & Leong, D. L. (1996). *Tools of the mind: A Vygotskian approach to early childhood education.* Englewood Cliffs, NJ: Merrill/Prentice Hall.

Boehm, A. E. (1992). Glossary of assessment terms. In L. R. Williams & D. P. Fromberg (Eds.), *Encyclopedia of early childhood education.* New York: Garland.

Boehm, A. E., & Weinberg, R. A. (1997). *The classroom observer: Developing observation skills in early childhood settings* (3rd ed.). New York: Teachers College Press.

Bolig, E. E., & Day, J. D. (1993). Dynamic assessment and giftedness: The promise of assessing training responsiveness. *Roeper Review, 16*(2), 110–113.

Bredekamp, S. (1987). *Developmentally appropriate practice in early childhood programs serving children from birth through age 8.* Washington, DC: National Association for the Education of Young Children.

Bredekamp, S., & Copple, C. (Eds.). (1997). *Developmentally appropriate practice in early childhood programs* (rev. ed.). Washington, DC: National Association for the Education of Young Children.

Bredekamp, S., & Rosegrant, T. (Eds.). (1992). *Reaching potentials: Appropriate curriculum and assessment for young children.* Washington, DC: National Association for the Education of Young Children.

Bricker, D., Pretti-Frontczak, K., & McComas, N. (1998). *An activity-based approach to early intervention.* Baltimore: P. H. Brookes.

Cadwell, L. B. (2002). *The Reggio Approach to early childhood education: Bring learning to life.* New York: Teachers College Press.

Cairns, H., & Hsu, J. R. (1978). Who, why, when, and how: A developmental study. *Journal of Child Langauge, 5,* 447–488.

Calhoon, J. M. (1997). Comparison of assessment results between a formal standardized measure and a play-based format. *Infant-Toddler Intervention: The Transdisciplinary Journal, 7*(3), 201–204.

Cartwright, G. A., & Cartwright, G. P. (1984). *Developing observational skills.* New York: McGraw-Hill.

Chen, J. (1998). *Project Spectrum: Early learning activities.* New York: Teachers College Press.

Chittenden, E. (1991). Authentic assessment, evaluation, and documentation of student performance. In V. Perrone (Ed.), *Expanding student assessment.* Alexandria, VA: Association for Supervision and Curriculum Development.

Cicchetti, D., & Wagner, S. (1990). Alternative assessment strategies for the evaluation of infants and toddlers: An organizational perspective. In S. J. Meisels & J. P. Shonkoff (Eds.), *Handbook of early childhood intervention* (pp. 246–277). New York: Cambridge University Press.

Clements, D. H., & Gullo, D. F. (1984). Effects of computer programming on young children's cognition. *Journal of Educational Psychology, 76*(6), 1051–1058.

Cleverley, J., & Phillips, D. C. (1986). *Visions of childhood: Influential models from Locke to Spock.* New York: Teachers College Press.

Cohen, L. G., & Spenciner, L. J. (1994). *Assessment of young children.* New York: Longman Press.

Cohen, L. G., & Spenciner, L. J. (2003). *Assessment of children and youth with special needs.* Boston: Allyn & Bacon.

Cole, D. J., Ryan, C. W., & Kick, F. (1995). *Portfolios across the curriculum and beyond.* Thousand Oaks, CA: Corwin Press.

Comer, J. P. (1999). Prologue—Child by child: The Comer process for change in education. In J. P. Comer, M. Ben-Avie, N. M. Haynes, & E. T. Joyner (Eds.), *Child by child: The Comer process for change in education* (pp. xix–xxvii). New York: Teachers College Press.

Comer, J. P., Haynes, N. M., & Joyner, E. T. (1996). The school development program. In J. P. Comer, N. M. Haynes, E. T. Joyner, & M. Ben-Avie (Eds.), *Rallying the whole village: The Comer process for reforming education* (pp. 1–26). New York: Teachers College Press.

Committee for Economic Development. (1991). *The unfinished agenda: A new vision for child development and education.* New York: Author.

Cryan, J. R. (1986). Evaluation: Plague or promise? *Childhood Education, 62*(5), 344–350.

Decker, C. A., & Decker, J. R. (1980). *Planning and administering early childhood programs* (2nd ed.). Columbus, OH: Merrill.

Deiner, P. L. (1993). *Resources for teaching children with diverse abilities.* Fort Worth, TX: Harcourt Brace Jovanovich.

Delclos, V. R. (1987). Effects of dynamic assessment on teachers' expecations of handicapped children. *American Educational Research Journal, 24*(3), 325–336.

Deno, S. L., Fuchs, L. S., Marston, D., & Shin, J. (2001). Using curriculum-based measurement to establish growth standards for students with learning disabilities. *School Psychology Review, 30*(4), 507–524.

Derman-Sparks, L. (1989). *Anti-bias curriculum: Tools for empowering young children.* Washington, DC: National Association for the Education of Young Children.

Diffily, D., & Fleege, P. O. (1994). The power of portfolios for communicating with families. *Dimensions of Early Childhood, 22*(2), 40–41.

Division for Early Childhood. (2000). *Developmental delay as an eligibility category.* DEC Position Paper. Missoula, MT: Council for Exceptional Children. Available online: http://www.dec-sped.org

Dunn, L., & Dunn, L. (1997). *PPVT-III: Peabody Picture Vocabulary Test* (3rd ed.). Circle Pines, MN: American Guidance Service.

Durkin, D. (1987). Testing in the kindergarten. *The Reading Teacher, 40*(8), 766–770.

Education Commission of the States (ECS). (2003). *Access to kindergarten: Age issues in state statutes.* Denver: Author.

Farmer-Dougan, V., & Kaszuba, T. (1999). Reliability and validity of play-based observations: Relationship between the PLAY Behaviour Observation System and the standardized measures of cognitive and social skills. *Educational*

Psychology: An International Journal of Experimental Educational Psychology, 19(4), 429–440.

Feuerstein, R. (1979). *The dynamic assessment of retarded performers: The learning potential assessment device, theory, instruments, and techniques.* Baltimore: University Park Press.

Feuerestein, R. (1980). *Instrumental enrichment.* Baltimore: University Park Press.

Fields, M. V., Groth, L. A., & Spangler, K. L. (2004). *Let's begin reading right: A developmental approach to emergent literacy.* Upper Saddle River, NJ: Pearson Merrill/Prentice Hall.

Fowler, S. A., Santos, R. M., & Corso, R. M. (Eds.). (2004). *Appropriate screening, assessment and family information gathering.* CLAS Collection No. 1. Longmont, CO: Sopris West.

Frank, C. (1999). *Ethnographic eyes: A teacher's guide to classroom observation.* Portsmouth, NH: Heinemann.

French, J. L., & Hale, R. I. (1990). A history of the development of psychological and educational testing. In C. R. Reynolds & R. W. Kamphaus (Eds.), *Handbook of psychological and educational assessment of children* (pp. 2–28). New York: Guilford Press.

Fuchs, L., & Deno, S. (1981). *The relationship between curriculum-based mastery measures and standardized achievement tests in reading* (Research Report No. 57). Minneapolis: University of Minnesota, Institute for Research on Learning Disabilities. (ERIC Document Reproduction Service No. ED212662)

Galagan, J. E. (1985). Psychoeducational testing: Turn out the lights, the party's over. *Exceptional Children, 52*(3), 288–299.

Gardner, H. (1983). *Frames of mind: The theory of multiple intelligences.* New York: Basic Books.

Gardner, H. (1999). *The disciplined mind: What all students should understand.* New York: Simon & Schuster.

Goodwin, W. R., & Driscoll, L. A. (1980). *Handbook for measurement and evaluation in early childhood education.* San Francisco: Jossey-Bass.

Goodwin, W. L., & Goodwin, L. D. (1982). Measuring young children. In B. Spodek (Ed.), *Handbook of research in early childhood education.* New York: Free Press.

Goodwin, W. L., & Goodwin, L. D. (1993). Young children and measurement: Standardized and nonstandardized instruments in early childhood education. In B. Spodek (Ed.), *Handbook of research on the education of young children* (pp. 441–463). New York: MacMillan.

Goodwin, W. L., & Goodwin, L. D. (1996). *Understanding quantitative and qualitative research in early childhood education.* New York: Teachers College Press.

Gonzalez-Mena, J. (1997). *Multicultural issues in child care* (2nd ed.). Mountain View, CA: Mayfield.

Gredler, G. R. (1984). Transition classes: A viable alternative for the at-risk child? *Psychology in the Schools, 21,* 463–470.

Guerin, G. R., & Maier, A. S. (1983). *Informal assessment in education.* Palo Alto, CA: Mayfield.

Gronlund, N. E. (1973). *Preparing criterion-referenced tests for classroom instruction.* New York: Macmillan.

Gullo, D. F. (1981). Social class differences in preschool children's comprehension of wh-questions. *Child Development, 52*(2), 736–740.

Gullo, D. F. (1982). A developmental study of low- and middle-class children's responses to wh-questions. *First Language, 3,* 211–221.

Gullo, D. F. (1988, November). *Perspectives on controversial issues related to implementing the all-day kindergarten: Evaluation and assessment.* Paper presented at the annual meeting of the National Association for the Education of Young Children, Anaheim, CA.

Gullo, D. F. (1992). *Developmentally appropriate teaching in early childhood: Curriculum, implementation, evaluation.* Washington, DC: National Educational Association.

Gullo, D. F. (1997). Assessing student learning through the analysis of pupil products. In B. Spodek & O. N. Saracho (Eds.), *Yearbook in early childhood education* (pp. 129–148). New York: Teachers College Press.

Gullo, D. F., & Ambrose, R. P. (1987). Perceived competence social acceptance in kindergarten: Its relationship to academic performance. *Journal of Educational Research, 8*(1), 28–32.

Gullo, D. F., Bersani, C., Clements, D. H., & Bayless, K. M. (1986). A comparative study of all-day, alternate-day, and half-day kindergarten schedules: Effects on achievement and classroom social behaviors. *Journal of Research in Childhood Education, 1*(2), 87–94.

Harms, T., Clifford, R. M., & Cryer, D. (1998). *Early Childhood Environment Rating Scale* (Rev. ed.). New York: Teachers College Press.

Harrington, H. L., Meisels, S. J., McMahon, P., Dichtelmiller, M. L., & Jablon, J. R. (1997). *Observing, documenting, and assessing learning: The work sampling system handbook for teacher educators.* Ann Arbor, MI: Rebus.

Hatch, T., & Gardner, H. (1996). If Binet had looked beyond the classroom: The assessment of multiple intelligences. *NAMTA Journal* (North American Montessori Teachers Association), *21*(2), 5–28.

Helm, J. H., Beneke, S., & Steinheimer, K. (1998). *Windows on learning: Documenting young children's work.* New York: Teachers College Press.

Herbert, E. A. (1992). Portfolios invite reflection—from students and staff. *Educational Leadership, 49*(8), 58–61.

Hoepfner, R., Stern, C., & Nummedal, S. (Eds.). (1971). *CSE-ECRC preschool/kindergarten test evaluations.* Los Angeles: University of California, Graduate School of Education.

Inhelder, B., Sinclair, H., & Bovet, M. (1974). *Learning and the development of cognition.* Cambridge, MA: Harvard University Press.

Irwin, D. M., & Bushnell, M. M. (1980). *Observational strategies for child study.* New York: Holt, Rinehart & Winston.

Jacobs, E. L. (2001). The effects of dynamic assessment components to a computerized preschool language screening test. *Communication Disorders Quarterly, 22*(4), 217–226.

Jitendra, A. K., & Kameenui, E. J. (1993). An exploratory study of dynamic assessment involving two instructional strategies on experts' and novices' performance in solving part-whole mathematical word problems. *Diagnostique, 18*(4), 305–325.

Jones, R. R. (1985). *The effect of a transition program on low achieving kindergarten students when entering first grade.* Unpublished doctoral dissertation. Northern Arizona University, Flagstaff.

Kelley, M. F., & Surbeck, E. (1983). Hisory of preschool assessment. In K. D. Paget & B. A. Bracken (Eds.), *The psychoeducational assessment of preschool children.* New York: Grune & Stratton.

Kemple, K. M. (2004). *Let's be friends: Peer competence and social inclusion in early childhood programs.* New York: Teachers College Press.

Kessen, W. (1965). *The child.* New York: John Wiley & Sons.

Kirkhart, K. (1995). Seeking multicultural validity: A postcard from the road. *Evaluation Practice, 16*(1), 1–12.

Kostelnik, M. J., Onaga, E., Rohde, B., & Whiren, A. (2002). *Children with special needs: Lessons for early childhood professionals.* New York: Teachers College Press.

Kostelnik, M., Soderman, A., & Whiren, A. (2004). *Developmentally appropriate curriculum: Best practices in early childhood education.* Upper Saddle River, NJ: Pearson/Merrill Prentice Hall.

Krechevsky, M. (1991). Project Spectrum: An innovative assessment alternative. *Educational Leadership, 49*(6), 43–48.

Krechevsky, M. (1998). *Project Spectrum: Preschool assessment handbook.* New York: Teachers College Press.

Krick, J. C. (1992). All children are special. In B. Neugebauer (Ed.), *Alike and different: Exploring our humanity with young children* (pp. 152–158). Washington, DC: National Association for the Education of Young Children.

Laosa, L. M. (1982). The sociocultural context of evaluation. In B. Spodek (Ed.), *Handbook of research in early childhood education* (pp. 501–520). New York: Free Press.

Lewis, A. (1995). An overview of the standards movement. *Phi Delta Kappan, 76*(10), 734–735.

Lidz, C. (1991). *Practitioner's guide to dynamic assessment.* New York: Guilford.

Lidz, C., & Pena, E. (1996). Dynamic assessment: The model, its relevance as a nonbiased approach, and its application to Latino American preschool children. *Language, Speech, and Hearing Services in the Schools, 27*(4), 367–372.

Lowenfeld, V., & Brittain, L. (1975). *Creative and mental growth.* New York: Macmillan.

Madaus, G. F. (1988). The influence of testing on the curriculum. In L. N. Tanner (Ed.), *Critical issues in the curriculum: 87th Yearbook of the National Society for the Study of Education.* Chicago: University of Chicago Press.

Madden, R., Gardner, E., & Collins, C. (1989). *Stanford Early Achievement Test* (3rd ed.). Cleveland: Psychological Corporation.

Malone, D. M. (1994). Contextual variation of correspondences among measures of play and developmental level of preschool children. *Journal of Early Intervention, 18*(2), 199–215.

Maness, B. J. (1992). Assessment in early childhood education. *Kappa Delta Pi Record, 28*(3), 77–79.

Markman, E. (1977). Realizing that you don't understand: A preliminary investigation. *Child Development, 48*(3), 286–292.

Marshall, H. (2003). Research in review: Opportunity deferred or opportunity taken? An updated look at delaying kindergarten entry. *Young Children, 58*(5), 84–93.

Maxwell, K., & Clifford, R. (2004). School readiness assessment. *Young Children, 59*(1), 42–46.

McAfee, O., & Leong, D. J. (2002). *Assessing and guiding young children's development and learning* (3rd ed.). Boston: Allyn & Bacon.

McCollum, J. A., & Maude, S. P. (1993). Portrait of a changing field: Policy and practice in early childhood special education. In B. Spodek (Ed.), *Handbook of research on the education of young children* (pp. 352–371). New York: Macmillan.

McLean, M. (1998, Spring). Assessing children for whom English is a second language. *Young Exceptional Children, 1*(3), 20–25.

McLean, M. (2000, September). *Conducting child assessments* (CLAS Technical Report No. 2). Champaign, IL: University of Illinois at Urbana-Champaign, Early Childhood Research Institute on Culturally and Linguistically Appropriate Services.

McLean, M., Smith, B. J., McCormick, K., Schakel, J., & McEvoy, M. (1991). *Developmental delay: Establishing parameters for a preschool category of exceptionality.* DEC Position Paper. Missoula, MT: Council for Exceptional Children.

Mehrens, W. A., & Lehmann, I. J. (1991). *Measurement and evaluation in education and psychology* (4th ed.). New York: Harcourt Brace.

Meisels, S. J. (1987). Uses and abuses of developmental screening and school readiness testing. *Young Children, 42*(4–6), 68–73.

Meisels, S. J. (1989). High-stakes testing in kindergarten. *Educational Leadership, 46*(7), 16–22.

Meisels, S.J. (1993). Remaking classroom assessment with the Work Sampling System. *Young Children, 48*(5), 34–40.

Meisels, S. J. (2000). On the side of the child: Personal reflections on testing, teaching, and early childhood education. *Young Children, 55*(5), 482–492.

Meisels, S. J., & Atkins-Burnett, S. (1994). *Developmental screening in early childhood: A guide.* Washington, DC: National Association for the Education of Young Children.

Meisels, S. J., & Atkins-Burnett, S. (2004). The Head Start National Reporting System: A critique. *Young Children, 59*(1), 64–66.

Meisels, S. J., et al. (2001). *The Work Sampling System* (4th ed.). Ann Arbor, MI: Rebus. Available online: http://www.pearsonearlylearning.com

Meisels, S. J., & Fenichel, E. (Eds.). (1996). *New visions for the developmental assessment of infants and young children.* Washington, DC: Zero to Three/National Center for Infants, Toddlers, and Families.

Meisels, S. J., & Steele, D. M. (1991). *Early Childhood Developmental Checklist* (Field Trial ed.). Ann Arbor, MI: University of Michigan.

Meisels, S. J., Wiske, M. S., & Tivnan, T. (1984). Predicting school performance with the Early Screening Inventory. *Psychology in the Schools, 21*(1), 25–33.

Mills, R. (1989). Portfolios capture rich array of student performance. *The School Administrator, 47*(10), 8–11.

Mindes, G. (2003). *Assessing young children* (2nd ed.). Upper Saddle River, NJ: Merrill/Prentice Hall.

Myers, C. L., McBride, S. L., & Peterson, C. A. (1996). Transdisciplinary, play-based assessment in early childhood special education: An examination of social validity. *Topics in Early Childhood Special Education, 16*(1), 102–126.

Nall, S. (1994). Assessment through portfolios in the all-day kindergarten. *National All-Day Kindergarten Network Newsletter, 4*(1), 1, 3.

National Association for the Education of Young Children (NAEYC). (1985). *National academy of early childhood programs.* Washington, DC: Author.

National Association for the Education of Young Children (NAEYC). (1988a). Position statement on standardized testing of young children 3 through 8 years of age. *Young Children, 43*(3), 42–47.

National Association for the Education of Young Children (NAEYC). (1988b). *Testing of young children: Concerns and cautions.* Washington, DC: Author.

National Association for the Education of Young Children (NAEYC). (1990). Guidelines for appropriate curriculum content and assessment in programs serving children ages 3 through 8. Washington, DC: Author.

National Association for the Education of Young Children (NAEYC). (2002*). Early learning standards: Creating the conditions for success* (Position Statement). Washington, DC: Author.

National Association for the Education of Young Children (NAEYC). (2003). *Early childhood curriculum, assessment, and program evaluation: Building an effective, accountable system in programs for children birth through age 8* (Position Statement). Washington, DC: Author.

National Association for the Education of Young Children (NAEYC). (2004). Where we stand: On curriculum, assessment, and program evaluation. *Young Children, 59*(1), 51–53.

National Association of State Boards of Education (NASBE). (1988). *Right from the start: The report of the National Assciation of State Boards of Education on early childhood education.* Alexandria, VA: Author.

National Association for Music Education. (1991). *Position Statement on Early Childhood Education.* Reston, VA: Author.

National Center for Education Statistics. (2002). *Digest of education statistics: 2001* (NCES 2002-031). Washington, DC: U.S. Department of Education, Office of Educational Research and Improvement.

Neisworth, J., & Bagnato, S. (1996). Assessment. In S. Odom & M. McLean (Eds.), *Early intervention/early childhood special education: Recommended practices.* Austin, TX: Pro-Ed.

Nicholls, J. (1978). The development of the concept of effort and ability, perceptions of academic attainment, and the understanding of difficult tasks that require more ability. *Child Development, 49,* 800–814.

Paulson, F. L., Paulson, P., & Meyer, C. (1991). What makes a portfolio? *Educational Leadership, 49*(5), 60–63.

Phillips, J. L (1975). *The origins of intellect: Piaget's theory.* San Francisco: W.H. Freeman.

Phillips, N., Fuchs, L. S., & Fuchs, D. (1994). Effects of classwide curriculum-based measurement and peer tutoring: A collaborative researcher-practitioner interview study. *Journal of Learning Disabilities, 27*(7), 420–434.

Phinney, J. S. (1982). Observing children: Ideas for teachers. *Young Children, 37*(5), 14–17.

Piaget, J. (1925). De quelques formes primitives de causalité chez l'enfant. *L'Année Psychologique, 26,* 31–71.

Piaget, J. (1963). *The origins of intelligence in children.* New York: Norton Library.

Ravitch, D. (1995). *National standards in American education.* Washington, DC: Brookings Institution.

Royce, J. M., Murray, H. W., Lazar, I., & Darlington, R. B. (1982). Methods of evaluating program outcomes. In B. Spodek (Ed.), *Handbook of research in early childhood education.* New York: Free Press.

Saluja, G., Scott-Little, C., & Clifford, R. (2000). Readiness for school: a survey of state policies and definitions. *Early Childhood Research and Practice, 2*(2). Available online: http://ecrp.uiuc.edu/v2n2/saluja.html

Santos, R. M. (2004). Ensuring culturally and linguistically appropriate assessment of young children. *Young Children, 59*(1), 48–50.

Scarr, S. (1976). An evolutionary perspective on infant intelligence: Species patterns and individual variations. In M. Lewis (Ed.), *Origins of intelligence: Infancy and early childhood* (pp. 165–198). New York: Plenum Press.

Schiff-Meyers, N. (1992). Considering arrested language development and language loss in the assessment of second language learners. *Language, Speech, and Hearing Services in the Schools, 23*(1), 28–33.

Schorr, L., & Schorr, D. (1988). *Within our reach: Breaking the cycle of poverty.* New York: Doubleday.

Schweinhart, L. J. (1988). *A school administrator's guide to early childhood programs.* Ypsilanti, MI: High/Scope Press.

Scott-Little, C., et al. (Eds.). (2003). *Assessing the state of state assessments: Perspectives on assessing young children.* Greensboro, NC: SERVE.

Sewell, M., Marczak, M., & Horn, M. (2003). *The use of portfolio assessment in evaluation.* Retrieved February 2, 2004, from http://ag.arizona.edu/fcr/fs/cyfar/Portfo~3htm

Shaklee, B. D., Barbour, N. E., Ambrose, R., & Hansford, S. J. (1997). *Designing and using portfolios.* Boston: Allyn & Bacon.

Shaklee, B. D., & Viechnicki, K. J. (1995). A qualitative approach to portfolios: The early assessment for exceptional children. *Journal for the Education of the Gifted, 18*(2), 156–170.

Shanklin, N., & Conrad, L. (1991). *Portfolios: A new way to assess student growth.* Denver: Colorado Council of the International Reading Association.

Shepard, L. (1989). Why we need better assessment. *Educational Leadership, 46*(7), 4–9.

Shepard, L., Kagan, S. L., & Wurtz, E. (Eds.). (1998). *Principles and recommendations for early childhood assessments* (National Education Goals Panel). Washington, DC: U.S. Government Printing Office.

Shepard, L. A., & Smith, M. L. (1985). *Boulder Valley kindergarten study: Retention practices and retention effects.* Boulder, CO: Boulder Valley Public Schools.

Shepard, L. A., & Smith, M. L. (1986). Synthesis of research on school readiness and kindergarten retention. *Educational Leadership, 44*(3), 78–86.

Shepard, L. A., & Smith, M. L. (1987). Effects of kindergarten retention at the end of first grade. *Psychology in the Schools, 24*(4), 346–357.

Shepard, L. A., & Smith, M. L. (1988). Escalating academic demand in kindergarten: Counterproductive policies. *The Elementary School Journal, 89*(2), 135–145.

Shore, R. (1998). *Ready schools: A report of the Goal 1 Ready Schools Resource Group.* Washington, DC: National Educational Goals Panel. Online: http://www.negp.gov/reports/readysch.pdf

Smith, M. L., & Glass, G. V. (1987). *Research and evaluation in education and the social sciences.* Englewood Cliffs, NJ: Prentice-Hall.

Spector, J. E. (1992). Predicting progress in beginning reading: Dynamic assessment of phonemic awareness. *Journal of Educational Psychology, 84*(3), 553–563.

Stein, J. U. (1993). Critical issues: Risk management, informed consent, and participant safety. In S. J. Grosse & D. Thompson (Eds.), *Leisure opportunities for individuals with disabilities: Legal issues* (pp. 37–54). Reston, VA: American Alliance for Health, Physical Education, Recreation, and Dance.

Stipek, D. J. (1981). Children's perceptions of their own and their classmates' ability. *Journal of Educational Psychology, 73*(3), 404–410.

Stipek, D. (2002). At what age should children enter kindergarten? A question for policy makers and parents. *Social Policy Report, 16*(2), 3–16. Available online: http://www.srcd.org/sprv16n2.pdf

Talan, T., & Bloom, P. J. (2005). *Program Administration Scale: Measuring early childhood leadership and management.* New York: Teachers College Press.

Tindal, G., & Marston, D. (1986). *Approaches to assessment: Psychoeducational perspectives on learning disabilities.* New York: Academic Press.

Tyack, D., & Ingram, D. (1977). Children's production and comprehension of questions. *Journal of Child Language, 4*(2), 211–224.

Uphoff, J., & Gilmore, J. E. (1986). *Summer children: Ready or not for school.* Middletown, OH: J & J Publishing.

U.S. Department of Education. (1991). *America 2000: An educational strategy source book.* Washington, DC: Author.

U.S. Department of Education. (2002a). *The facts about . . . measuring progress.* U.S. Department of Education. Retrieved July 16, 2002, from http://www.ed.gov/nclb/accountability/ayp/testing.html

U.S. Department of Education. (2002b). *The No Child Left Behind Act of 2001: Executive Summary.* U.S. Department of Education. Retrieved July 16, 2002, from http://www.ed.gov/nclb/overview/intro/execsumm.html

Valencia, R. R., & Suzuki, L. A. (2001). *Intelligence testing and minority students: Foundations, performance factors, and assessment.* Thousand Oaks, CA: Sage.

VanDerHeyden, A. M., Witt, J. C., Naquin, G., & Noell, G. (2001). The reliability and validity of curriculum-based measurement readiness probes for kindergarten students. *School Psychology Review, 30*(3), 363–382.

Van de Walle, J. A. (2004). *Elementary and middle school mathematics: Teaching developmentally.* Boston: Pearson.

Van Hoorn, J., Nourot, P., Scales, B., & Alward, K. (1999). *Play at the center of the curriculum*. Upper Saddle, NJ: Merrill/Prentice Hall.

Vasta, R. (1979). *Studying children*. San Francisco: Freeman.

Vavrus, L. (1990, August). Put portfolios to the test. *Instructor, 99,* 48–51.

Vermont Department of Education. (1988). *Working together to show results: An approach to school accountability for Vermont*. Montpelier, VT: Author.

Vermont Department of Education. (1989). *Vermont writing assessment: The portfolio*. Montpelier, VT: Author.

Vialle, W. (1994). Profiles of intelligence. *Australian Journal of Early Childhood Education, 19*(4), 30–34.

Vygotsky, L. (1978). *Mind in society: The development of higher psychological processes*. (M. Cole, V. John-Steiner, S. Scribner, & E. Souberman, Eds.). Cambridge, MA: MIT Press.

Vygotsky, L. (1986). *Thought and language* (A. Kozulin, Trans.). Cambridge, MA: MIT Press.

Webster, R., McInnis, E., & Carver, L. (1986). Curriculum biasing effects in standardized and criterion-referenced reading achievement tests. *Psychology in the Schools, 23*(2), 205–213.

Wexler-Sherman, C., Gardner, H., & Feldman, D. H. (1988). A pluralistic view of early assessment: The Project Spectrum approach. *Theory into Practice, 27*(1), 77–83.

White, S. H. (1973). *Federal programs for young children: Review and recommendations (Vol. 13)*. Washington, DC: Government Printing Office.

Wiener, R. B., & Cohen, J. H. (1997). *Literacy portfolios: Using assessment to guide instruction*. Upper Saddle River, NJ: Merrill/Prentice Hall.

Wiggins, G. (1996). What is a rubric? A dialogue on design and use. In R. E. Blum & J. A. Arter (Eds.), *Student performance assessment in an era of restructuring* (pp. VI-5:1–VI-5:13). Alexandria VA: Association for Supervision and Curriculum Development.

Wiske, M. S., Meisels, S. J., & Tivnan, T. (1981). The Early Screening Inventory: A study of early childhood developmental screening. In N. J. Anastasiow, W. K. Frankenburg, & A. Fandel (Eds.), *Identification of high risk children*. Baltimore: University Park Press.

Wolery, M. (1994). Assessing children with special needs. In M. Wolery & J. S. Wilbers (Eds.), *Including children with special needs in early childhood programs* (pp. 71–96). Washington, DC: National Association for the Education of Young Children.

Wolery, M., Strain, P. S., & Bailey, D. B. (1992). Reaching potentials of children with special needs. In S. Bredekamp & T. Rosegrant (Eds.), *Reaching potentials: Appropriate curriculum and assessment for young children* (pp. 92–112). Washington, DC: National Association for the Education of Young Children.

Wolery, M., & Wilbers, J. S. (Eds.) (1994). *Including children with special needs in early childhood programs*. Washington, DC: National Association for the Education of Young Children.

Wortham, S. C. (1990). *Tests and measurement in early childhood education*. Columbus, OH: Merrill.

Wortham, S. C. (2001). *Assessment in early childhood education.* Upper Saddle River, NJ: Merrill/Prentice Hall.

Worthen, B. R., & Spandel, V. (1991). Putting the standardized test debate in perspective. *Educational Leadership, 48*(5), 65–69.

Yansen, E., & Shulman, E. (1996). Language assessment: Multicultural considerations. In L. Suzuki, P. Meller, & J. Ponterotto (Eds.), *The handbook of multicultural assessment* (pp. 353–393). San Francisco: Jossey-Bass.

Zigler, E., & Valentine, J. (1979). *Project Head Start: A legacy of the War on Poverty.* New York: Free Press.

Index

About the Author

DOMINIC GULLO is a professor of elementary and early childhood education at Queens College, City University of New York. He is also a member of the doctoral faculty at the City University of New York Graduate Center. He received his doctorate from Indiana University in the Interdisciplinary Doctoral Program on Young Children. Before becoming a professor, he taught for 5 years in the public schools at the prekindergarten and kindergarten levels. He was also a teacher in the Head Start program. At Queens College, he teaches courses in assessment, early language and literacy, and curriculum at the prekindergarten and kindergarten levels. He is a consultant to school districts around the country in early childhood education, language and literacy, and assessment. He serves on numerous national boards, and is currently on the governing board of the National Association for the Education of Young Children. He is the author of three books, two early childhood curriculums, and over 75 research-based publications. He has presented his work both nationally and internationally.